THE CHARRED WOOD

BLESSED JULIE BILLIART

THE CHARRED WOOD

THE STORY OF BLESSED JULIE BILLIART

*Foundress of the Congregation
of
Sisters of Notre Dame of Namur*

by

MALACHY GERARD CARROLL

ILLUSTRATED BY A SISTER OF NOTRE DAME

SANDS & CO. (Publishers) LTD.
London   Glasgow

Nihil obstat: ROMANUS RIOS, Ab. O.S.B.
CENSOR DEPUTATUS
Imprimatur: HUBERTUS GIBNEY
VIC. GEN.
Southwarci, die 19a Julii, 1950.

Made and printed in Great Britain by
Northumberland Press Limited, Gateshead on Tyne

AUTHOR'S PREFACE

I HAVE called this book the Story of Blessed Julie Billiart, and in my use of original documents, letters and already published works, I have been concerned principally with those things which served to fix the lines of her character. It is, therefore, but incidentally a story of the early years of Notre Dame, and does not contain a chapter on the spread of the Institute.

All biographical detail is carefully drawn from a manuscript, *Vie de la Bienheureuse Mère Julie Billiart*, written by the co-Foundress. I have also consulted the following works: *La Vénérable Mère Julie Billiart*, by P. Ch. Clair, S.J., and the two English works based on it. Also *Histoire de la Vénérée Mère Saint Joseph*—a work which is a model of its kind.

I wish to thank Miss Maureen Callaghan for patient co-operation in preparing the manuscript for the Press.

M.G.C.

CONTENTS

LIST OF ILLUSTRATIONS

9

FOREWORD

SOMEONE has said that if saints were ever lacking in any generation, they would have to be invented. Fortunately the situation cannot arise, but if saints had to be invented to suit the spiritual needs of the present generation we have, in the life of Blessed Julie Billiart, a perfect blue-print of the kind of thing that is wanted. Corresponding to our own times of turbulence and disintegration were the years of Blessed Julie's life-long struggles for the mastery of the spiritual over the material. In coming to Christ through such barricades as the French Revolution and the free-thinking decades which followed, the Foundress of the Congregation of Sisters of Notre Dame performed a work of personal sanctification which must appeal to souls who find it hard to come to Him in an age when the obstacles are those evils which inevitably attend the totalitarian theory.

But Julie Billiart did more than merely sanctify her own soul in a climate which one would have judged to be inimical to sanctity: by her interpretation of religious upbringing she effected a minor social revolution of her own. Without apparently any very clear programme beforehand, she so co-operated with the moment-to-moment unfolding of God's plan as to become an innovator in education, a religious foundress, a woman of enormous spiritual influence upon her generation. Founders and reformers are of two kinds: there are those whose preconceived ideas about a particular ideal or need drive them to the realization

of their vocation, and there are those who find themselves ending up as founders and reformers because all
along they have simply wanted God and souls. Blessed
Julie was of this latter kind. For one thing it was com-
paratively late in life that she began to bear any sort
of outward fruit to her perfection. For nearly twenty
years of her adult life she was a cripple. Her powers
of speech were such that it was only with difficulty that
she could be understood. She suffered from some kind
of nervous complaint which made administration, and
even sustained correspondence, if not impossible, at
least very difficult. It was only when she had been
miraculously cured of her many infirmities that the
community which had gathered itself around her was
able to feel that it had at last a substance and shape.
Petty persecution—and on occasion not so petty—was
her lot through life; again and again the misunderstandings with ecclesiastical superiors, which seem to be
inseparable from the story of all religious foundations,
threatened to destroy her work; disappointments arising from temperamental Sisters under her care, from
the short-sighted policies of local superiors, from sudden
failures in health and funds, from the estrangement of
friends and even from the malice of the devil: this was
the stuff of Blessed Julie's life. "Shaped under the hard
blows of blunted tools," the finished product was surely
a work of God's art.

Several impressions of startling clarity must remain
with anyone who has read this book. After the curious
picture of ecclesiastical supervision to which the devout
were subject in those days, there is the awareness in the
reader's mind throughout the narrative—an awareness
which is substantiated by documentary quotation—of
the part played by the co-Foundress, Mère Blin. It is
to be hoped that a full-length life will one day be
written of this remarkable servant of God. With a
completely different background from Blessed Julie's,

Françoise Blin came to her vocation from a family of wealth and tradition. Her devotion to the Foundress is as touching as it is sane and practical: Mère Blin makes her written contribution to the annals of the Congregation in a style which is at once literary and matter-of-fact, and reading between the lines one may discover what it was that drew the older woman, with her origins in the humble Picardy home, towards this outstanding and yet self-effacing soul. The two religious shared the same spirit from the start—the spirit which was to animate the Congregation of Notre Dame. If it was a quality of Blessed Julie that "she thought in straight lines," it was Mère Blin's gift that her lines ran parallel.

The third conception which emerges unmistakably from the study of Blessed Julie's *Story* is that of the central figure as a soul of prayer. This is only what you would expect, but it is at the same time the most important feature in the book. Trained in prayer during the long years that she spent on her back, Blessed Julie was granted supernatural favours which must rank high in the history of mystical experience. The gift of levitation was witnessed by others, and she herself speaks of the vision which she had of future members of her religious family. Four or five hours in prayer a day was apparently a not unusual amount of time to give to the most worthwhile occupation of the soul, and though she found the same attraction to contemplative prayer that she saw among the Carmelites, with whom she was associated for a short time during the early part of her career, Blessed Julie was far from being the leisured mystic. There were journeys to make, Bishops to call on, houses to buy and move into, conferences to give, brigands and thieves to escape from (with supernatural assistance), and schools to open for "a hundred and thirty-two children" when nothing was ready for them, and the Foundress herself had to "go out collecting a stove, a saucepan, a gridiron." In Blessed Julie's correspondence we get remarks about her having to "beat the town for a house," about her having to settle down for the night in a room with no candles and "a few faggots found in the corner to serve as pillows," about "accepting a jug of beer" from an innkeeper, and about being, in conditions of extreme poverty, "the happiest people in Ghent."

If recollection can be maintained in the midst of all this, there is evidence enough for the belief that Blessed Julie's vocation was neither completely contemplative nor strictly active. In the mixed life the Notre Dame vocation finds its full perfection. "The next two days were very busy ones for Julie, but she was one of those people who have the rare gift of getting things done thoroughly, quickly, quietly, without surrounding themselves and everyone and everything with a fog of fuss": this is not a citation from the annals, but it is a passage taken from the present work. There are comments in these pages which point in the same direction and which give—if an outsider like myself may venture an opinion—the authentic note of the Congregation's spirit. Not exclusively cause, not exclusively effect, the secret of Notre Dame of Namur is simplicity. Simplicity in prayer, in manner of life, in outlook. It is the Gospel spirit after all, and if you like you can call it the life of faith. It also goes by the name of charity. But in any case, it is the essence of the religious vocation—as nobody could have seen more clearly than Blessed Julie Billiart, Foundress of the Congregation of the Sisters of Notre Dame of Namur.

In conclusion, I hope it will not be considered an impertinence to add a word of congratulation upon the author's handling of the material. This book could easily have been an echo of many such edifying lives. Mr. Carroll, however, has given an individuality to the text which is worthy of the subject. Selection, accuracy, and sympathy are the three things most required in a biographer, and Mr. Carroll has clearly been to infinite pains to express all three; that he has managed to do so, and at the same time to preserve the flavour of originality, is an achievement for a writer of religious biography.

DOM HUBERT VAN ZELLER, O.S.B.

July, 1950.

" Ah, must Thou char the wood
Ere Thou canst limn with it?"
FRANCIS THOMPSON.

" Is the object of life only to live?
Will the feet of God's children be
Fastened to this wretched earth?
It is not to live, but to die, and not to
Hew the cross, but to mount upon it, and to
Give all that we have, laughing!"
PAUL CLAUDEL.

EVENING IN CUVILLY

LEGEND

✠ Cuvilly
1 Beauvais
2 Compiegne
3 Ressons
4 Mondidier
5 St. Ouen

6 Amiens
7 Paris
8 Calais
9 Namur
10 Ghent

11 Brussels
12 Dinant
13 St. Hubert
14 Jumet
15 Binche

"PLAYING" AT TEACHING THEM ABOUT GOD

CHAPTER ONE

WHERE PEACE COMES DROPPING

SHADOWS were lengthening in Cuvilly, a little village of Picardy with the face of an old man whom time has passed by and forgotten. You knew the wisdom in that face, and you knew the silence that came dropping with the sunset, breathing peace on broken earth and cobbled street. At the entrance to the village, the scent of roses perfumed the air about the wayside crucifix. The crucifix with its wealth of greens and roses, made a pool of shadow on the road. The top and arm-beam were clear in the tangle of shadow. A market cart rumbled its way through that tangle, and for a second, the cross lay on man and beast. You thought of life: pretty much of a tangled shadow, really, with the shadow of the cross flung upon it as the answer to its riddle.

Pools of darkness soon began to settle on Cuvilly and shadow flowed into shadow. The face of Cuvilly—the old man's face—was heavy with the shadows of sleep.

There was a great peace in those shadows, yet was the shadow of the cross there, too. Just as it was on every village in Picardy, on the night-shadowed roof of every house, on the deeps in every human soul. Just as it lay on the swarming heart of Paris, dizzy with the din of its desires. For the cross lies on every threshold, to be shouldered daily. It lies in the shadows about the feet of all men, to become an exaltation or a stumbling-block. The cross is measured by the grace that is given: but every man is born to be crucified.

Evening in Cuvilly could bring thoughts like these—

thoughts of shadow, an old man's meditation. The
sunset, for all its beauty and silence, can be a laugh of
scorn at the heaped-up vanities of life, and can bring
to birth that precious moment when man is brought to
a deep heart and God is glorified.

Monsieur l'Abbé Dangicourt, Curé of Cuvilly, pon-
dered many things, as he stood looking through the
window of his little house. There was a kindly softness
about the face, a face that was pencilled in firm yet soft
lines on which, you knew, no human soul could tear
itself. The peace of the man's soul was in his quiet
eyes. The Parish of Cuvilly knew those eyes upon it
like the blessing of God. Piety, zeal, learning, an
ecclesiastic of rare merit, these were the words that
were spoken in high places of Monsieur l'Abbé. His
people knew him as a man of prayer: they said that
when he breathed, his breath was prayer. They loved
him for his gentleness and his prayer, because the smile
of Christ's grace was in his love for them. Standing at
his window, he watched the houses beginning to huddle
together more closely as twilight deepened, and he felt
in the whole scene the thought and the rhythm of the
Vesper prayer that was drifting through his mind:

> " O Blest Creator of the Light,
> Who, gently blending eve with morn,
> And morn with eve, didst call them day;
> Thick flows the flood of darkness down;
> Oh, hear us, as we weep and pray."

Monsieur l'Abbé knew much about the tears of life,
for a good priest is one who can sympathize even with
the silly stupidities of human nature, cutting itself
with the briars of its own wilfulness, no less than with
the tares of life's great sorrows. He knew the laugh
of the grace of God in human nature, too: the courage,
the heroism, the beauty buried in the daily life of his

people, a life outwardly as dull as the soil they tilled.
He knew the Magnificat intoned in his own soul when,
in the dull routine of life, he met with souls whose
eyes were fixed on grace-swept horizons. To-day, that
Magnificat had been loud in his soul: to-day, it had
been given him to look into the white depths of a child's
soul, and to realize fully—he had long suspected it—
that he had been given the awful charge of forming a
saint. That child was Marie-Rose-Julie Billiart. It
seemed but yesterday that baby had been carried to
him, and yet it was nine years ago, in 1751, and he had
christened her Marie-Rose. . . . To-day, it had been
given to him to know the soul of this child whose per-
fume was making lovely the spiritual garden of his
parish: to realize how beautifully this child was beginning to live her name.

Monsieur l'Abbé knew and praised God for the
splendid spirituality he found in the home of the
Billiarts. Four little coffins had been carried over
the threshold of that home in but a few years, as child
after child had died. "Rachael bewailing her children
and would not be comforted because they are not":
these words came to the good priest as he looked at the
young mother and knew the bitterness of her sorrow.
He told her that the infinite Wisdom of God can do
nothing pointless and stupid: that there is a divine
loving plan behind the sending of every cross: that it
would all add up to a great grace. . . . Meantime, a
child had been born to them. They took the name that
had been written on the second little coffin—Marie-
Rose. Their first Marie-Rose had been taken away
while yet the splendour of her Baptismal innocence
was one with the whiteness of the angels. It was a
delicate thought of Monsieur l'Abbé, that something of
this angelic light had pierced the darkness of the grave
and taken the soul of her sister as with a zephyr of
light, when the name of Marie-Rose-Julie was spoken

over another child of Jean-Françoise Billiart and Marie-Louise-Antoinette Debraine. For Monsieur l'Abbé was convinced that the crosses had added up to the gift of an angelically pure and simple child.

To-day he had taken a decision about that child, a decision which would have caused great concern and heart-searching to most of his fellow clergy. In eighteenth-century France, the chill fingers of Jansenism were on the Blessed Eucharist, and the dust of false reverence and misguided humility was clogging the stream of sacramental grace. It seems strange to us to-day, that a child should not be allowed to make her First Communion till the age of fourteen: yet this was so in the eighteenth century. Little Julie Billiart was only nine, but Monsieur l'Abbé had evidence that her age was not to be reckoned by man's years. He had heard how the child would slip off to a quiet corner of her home to pray: he had seen her slipping away from her companions to visit the church: he had followed her and had secretly watched her in prayer. It troubled him that a soul which the Holy Ghost was so obviously shaping to His image should be denied the Body and Blood of Christ. Yet custom is a strong dictator, and Monsieur l'Abbé hesitated.

He consulted the village schoolmaster, Thibault Guilbert, who was Julie's uncle. Thibault was one of the pillars of Cuvilly society: he was "the master," walking his life among a simple people, with the whisper of his learning about him. When the good people of Cuvilly, tired from toiling in field and kitchen, gathered in the evening round their Curé in the fine old church to praise God, it was "the master" who intoned the hymn which followed the prayers. The prayers said were the "Night Prayers of the late Monseigneur the Marshal of Bellefont," and the manuscript from which they were read was in the bold, clear hand of "the master," with a flourishing signature and this charmingly pedantic little note: "The late Cardinal de Bouillon thought them so beautiful that he wished to have them for use in his own home. It is certain that anyone who reads them slowly will find them full of unction." . . . A man, then, whose opinion on any matter in Cuvilly was placed second only to that of Monsieur l'Abbé himself. If Monsieur l'Abbé and "the master" spoke together, the air was humming with wisdom about the heads of the good people of Cuvilly. The priest had brought his problem about Julie to Thibault. The master had said that, while the child was natural and unobtrusive, there yet was something "different" about her. Of course she was intelligent, but her level of intelligence did not explain her amazing zeal for and mature grasp of the Catechism and of Sacred Scripture. Already, she could quote a lot of Scripture by heart. Had Monsieur l'Abbé heard her "playing" at teaching religion to her companions? And had Monsieur l'Abbé noticed who these companions were: the poor who could not come to school, the beggar waif and stray?

Monsieur l'Abbé had seen the wonder for himself today. He had watched and listened to the child, as she sat in the midst of her companions on a grassy slope, "playing" at teaching them about God. The clearness of her exposition, her contagious enthusiasm and sincerity amazed the good priest. She was speaking to them about the grace of God, and she had prepared her stage for her story. Monsieur l'Abbé could see, from where some bushes concealed him, that part of the soil had been dug up with a stick that now lay clay-coated on the grass, that a handful of pebbles had been strewn beside the broken soil, and that the soil on the other side had small thorn branches stuck in it. "The sower went out to sow his seed": the child suited her actions to her story, sowing little handfuls of seed, while her companions watched her, entranced with the story. The

explanation and the exhortation were perfect: and
Monsieur l'Abbé found himself murmuring: "*Ex ore
infantium*," and he knew the joy of a Magnificat in his
soul. Then voices were heard calling the children
home, the little "game" finished, and the child said
to her companions with unaffected simplicity:

"Bring the ones who were not here to-night for next
time, won't you? I want plenty of little souls, to teach
them how to love and serve the good God."

"*Magnificat anima mea Dominum*," sang the heart
of Monsieur l'Abbé as he stepped out on the path. In
one of those swift moments of intuition which mock the
tardy feet and fears of prudence, he called the child to
him and asked her if she would like to receive Holy
Communion. The face that was suddenly lifted to him
with the shock of surprise, was transfigured for a second
with radiant joy, before the natural shyness of the child
showed itself in her blushes, her deep curtsey and her
whispered: "Yes, if Monsieur l'Abbé allows me."
Monsieur l'Abbé had seen that joy and it had been a
visible sign to him of the approval of Heaven. He
placed his hand gently on her head, and told her his
wish that she should receive Holy Communion on the
greater Feasts of the Church. She must tell her father
and mother only, and not speak to her companions
about it. Would she promise him that? Again he saw
the radiance in her face and heard her whispered
answer. Her little hand was nervously clutching her
dress. He noticed how it was leaving a clay-stain on
the dress—the clay of her parable.

"But secretly, for fear of the Jews": the words came
to his mind as he watched the child hurrying away
towards her home. Things had come to a strange pass
indeed, when such secrecy was necessary in order that
one might co-operate with the Holy Ghost in fashion-
ing a child's soul to His image.

Night was beginning to pile itself against the window

of his house, as Monsieur l'Abbé stood there deep in thought about this child.   Prayer was suffusing that thought: prayer for light to guide a soul so obviously loved by God that the crosses of His chastisements must surely await her at every turning of her life.   Still thinking and planning for this soul, Monsieur l'Abbé turned from the window to his shadow-draped room, stirred his fire to life and lighted his lamp.   He looked along one row of his books, and selected a copy of the *Imitation of Christ*.   He would give it to the child.   He knew no better book for the beginnings and the heights of sanctity, apart from the Bible itself.

Thus was the shaping of the soul of Julie Billiart begun.   There was nothing soft or effeminate about that shaping, for she, who was to tell her followers later to be *men*, was herself cast in the mould of a man.   Monsieur l'Abbé Dangicourt saw to that.   He knew that all sanctity must be based on self-restraint, for it was with hard blows only that a soul could be shaped to the tremendous vocation of Julie Billiart.   When the years are folded back on the magnificent achievement of this woman, a child is revealed, kneeling alone in the icy dawn-coldness of a stone church, her head bowed fervently on her Eucharistic Lord.   From this came the simplicity, the meekness, the humility, and the iron determination of the woman.   Whether the secret of her furtive union with her God was kept or not, we do not know.   But its effects could not be kept secret, so that before long all Cuvilly was speaking of little Julie Billiart as "the saint."

Anyone in Cuvilly could have told you where to find Jean-François Billiart, for when a family is as long in a townland as the Billiarts were in Cuvilly, you enquire about its members much as you might enquire about a local hill or stream.   There were always Billiarts in Cuvilly, the oldest villager will tell you, and if you have time to listen, he will trace the line back and back and

back. You will gather that the Billiarts were once
people of considerable property, who knew the secret
of carrying their possessions across the clay of the grave:
aye, ask the Curé about that, for he knows how often
the name Billiart has figured on subscription lists to
church and charity: there was a Billiart, too—he will
go on to tell you—who was a "lieutenant de justice" for
these parts: and so, in the leisurely way of an old man's
musings, you will come to Jean-François Billiart. The
old man will linger on the name as he says it, with that
peculiar combination of speaking and tasting which
indicates that the name is a gracious one to the speaker.
You will hear that, while Jean-François has no abun-
dance of this world's goods, he has sufficient to make
him "passing rich" in the community of Cuvilly. His
plot of land, by comparison with the lands of the seven-
teenth-century Billiarts, is indeed only a few handfuls
of soil, but a few handfuls of the best soil in Picardy
given to a few of the most industrious people in Cuvilly.
For it isn't only Jean-François who works to gain as rich
a yield as his plot can give: there is his wife, and there
are his children. . . . Once again, you get the sensa-
tion that the man is appreciatively tasting each name.
On your way up the street, he goes on, you must have
passed a little draper's shop with the name Billiart
above the window. That is a venture of Jean-François,
and he seems to be doing quite well. You do remember
watching a man putting up his shutters as you passed.

Your curiosity aroused, perhaps you follow the old
man's directions, and walk the seven minutes that bring
you from the church to the home of the Billiarts. You
go along a narrow country lane, and you pause by a
little gate in a moss-green wall. A small, uneven yard;
a long, low, thatched cottage; a fence and some flowers.
As you watch, a little girl comes out, fills a basin from
the water-barrel, and returns to the house. This must
be the child, Marie-Rose-Julie, whose name you had

THE JOY OF ONE WHO HAS BEEN INVITED TO THE
WEDDING-FEAST

heard spoken with an old man's reverence. It is quite
dusk now. You cannot see the joy that makes that
young face lovely. The joy of one who has just been
invited to the Wedding-Feast.

The child had known the fulness of her joy as she
hastened away from her conversation with Monsieur
l'Abbé. She had run eagerly up the lane and into the
little kitchen where her mother was preparing a meal.
Breathless, the words tumbling over one another, she
told her wonderful news. Her mother embraced and
kissed her, and for a long minute she looked at her
child. Then she said quietly:

"It is a big gift, Julie, and don't let it make you
think you are better than anyone else. You must keep
your secret, and let your secret make you a good girl.
Come, now, wash these dishes for me. You'll find hot
water in the kettle."

Thank heaven for the daily, matter-of-fact remark
that can keep one from showing the tears that suddenly
gather in one's eyes. In that long minute in which
she had looked at her child, many things had come to
her mind. The faces of her other children seemed in
that face—the children she had laid, each in its own
little coffin, when the dryness of sorrow was in her soul.
She had heard in that minute, too, the echo of Monsieur l'Abbé's words: "It will add up to a great grace."
In that long minute she had seen that grace and the joy
of that grace in the face of her child.

Devotion to the Sacred Heart was the great central
candle of devotion set up by this good mother in the
midst of her family life and in the souls of her children.
When both mother and child had gone to their reward,
this devotion could still be found deep in the heart of
every Billiart. In a magnificent extension, it was and
is to be found in the spirit of Notre Dame. For this
child was to grow into the Foundress who would gather
her fervent followers about the tabernacle every even-

ing to recite in common an Act of Reparation to the Sacred Heart of Jesus. Her followers still gather for this Act of Reparation. It is well to remember that behind that living Act of Reparation, there is both the sublime fervour of the Foundress of Notre Dame and the simple piety of a simple mother who knew how to enthrone the Sacred Heart in the heart of her child. A book remains to be written on the mothers of the saints, for—while the Monicas have received their meed of praise—the Marie-Louise-Antoinette Debraines are too lightly passed over.

There is something exquisitely personal about drops of wax on old parchment. A human hand has written the words, human eyes have read those words in the yellow, flickering light of a candle, and a drop of wax has fallen with something of the warmth of charity in its heart. It has settled there like the image of a warm prayer that is said, and whose impress, like the wax, may still be mysteriously in some human soul. . . . The Sisters of Notre Dame treasure a little manual of prayer which was used in the parish church of Cuvilly when their Foundress was a child there. The book opens readily at a well-fingered prayer celebrating the depth of love in the Divine Eucharistic Heart of Christ, and there are drops of wax on the page. It is a fact worthy of notice that the prayer of Reparation said every Tuesday in the Order of Notre Dame is this prayer from the age-mellowed Cuvilly manual. That prayer has come to Notre Dame through the souls of hundreds of the simple people who knelt and prayed with a child they called their "saint." The devotion to the Sacred Heart that radiated from the church at Cuvilly three centuries ago, that was cast as fire and enkindled as fire in the heart of a mother and child, has come as a precious legacy to thousands who are striving to model their lives after the example of that child. The loom of God weaves wonderful things: a simple thread may be the beginning of a magnificent design. Behind that tremendous realization of an ideal that is the Institute of the Sisters of Notre Dame, there is found the heroic intrepidity of a woman who found her strength in keeping the soul of a child. That is indeed true. But the faith of a mother who knew her child as a grace from heaven, is there also.

Marie-Louise-Antoinette Debraine guessed nothing of the designs of God for her child. She was a very busy woman, for there were the house and the meals, and the fowl, and the plot, and the garden. Yes, as she glanced at the picture of the Sacred Heart she had hung on the kitchen wall, she fell to thinking the long, long thoughts of a mother and she sighed that sigh of tenderness and of hope, which is the single, unfathomable sign given to a gross world, of the sacred deeps of a mother's heart, where her hopes and fears nestle, and where she keeps them all, pondering them.

CHAPTER TWO

CROSSES AND BEGINNINGS

CHRIST entered heaven, says St. Gregory of Nyssa, with His bride, Humanity, whom He espoused upon the Cross. The music that accompanied the nuptials of Humanity and Divinity was, therefore, the sound of iron on iron, piercing flesh: the nuptial garment was woven of blood and pain, and the feet of the Beloved were beautiful because they were wet from the winepress.

The sound of that hammer, rising and falling, has filled the world of Christian souls, and will continue to be the authentic voice of that world till the end of time. God became man, that man might become as God: the Incarnation has its full meaning in that it is the way to final transfiguration and deification. The way . . . Christ said "I am the way." The same way, the only way, a way with pain in it, with blood upon its stones, with the steady clang of the crucifying hammer in its heat and its dust: yet—splendid paradox —a way in which there is joy.

The sorrows and trials of life must, however lightly, leave the spiritual imprint of the nails upon the Christain soul, for only thus can it reach its transfiguration. But when God makes special choice of a soul, such spiritual imprint will not be slight: He looks upon such a soul from His Cross, that the light of His agonized countenance may be upon it, and that He may mark it with a sign. Sorrow and darkness and pain will be the world of such a soul: it will shoulder its cross in the darkness of its way, and will walk the winepress of its suffering until its feet are red with the blood of its pain. It will drag its cross, and there will be a strange joy in the dragging—a joy that becomes ecstasy when it stumbles, in the evening, to the Hill where its cross becomes one with the Cross of Christ, and where Christ espouses His beloved in the crowning of a cross. Of such a soul, a great modern poet[1] has said magnificently:

> " Heart that achieved such a fervour of springing and
> singing
> When life locked it up in a cellar away from the light,
> O, how it gathered its strength in the gloom for more
> wonderful winging,
> And rose and rejoiced like a star in that fullness of
> night."

When Marie-Rose-Julie Billiart was leaving the church after having received the Sacrament of Confirmation, one of the Knights Hospitallers of St. John of Jerusalem gave her an authentic relic of the true Cross, set in a large cruciform reliquary and labelled: "Given to Julie Billiart by a Knight of Malta." The gift was a splendid index to the respect in which the child was held. But it was more than that. . . . Put it this way. The seamless garment of young life, minute woven into minute, should be a thing of white loveliness, unshadowed with the greys and the browns of pain. Life had been so for Julie Billiart, in the noiseless flow of Cuvilly minutes, up to the time of her Confirmation. Our metaphor suggests weaving, and it has a special appropriateness here, for there is a sense in which this child can be said to have woven her own thoughts. She certainly wove white thoughts about the Mother of God into a silk banner of hers, venerated in the Mother House of Notre Dame in Namur, and bearing the inscription: "Thou art all fair, O Mary, and there

---

[1] Rainer Maria Rilke (trans. Leishman).

is no stain in thee"—every letter the labour of a child's love. She wove these thoughts into a Christ-thought, when a year later, with the permission of Monsieur l'Abbé Dangicourt, she vowed her virginity to God. "I have come to cast fire on the earth," said Christ: and where it kindled intensely, it glowed white with the whiteness of virgin purity. In the warm strength of that whiteness, God fashions the eyes that shall see God. We say *warm* whiteness, for there is nothing of the chill of Grecian marble about the Christian idea of chastity: it is the whiteness of the white heat of charity cast by Christ upon the earth, and only as such is it blessed. Julie Billiart took a vow of virginity a year after her Confirmation: the whiteness of her soul was lifted, defenceless, to the purity of God. The Knight who gave her a splinter of the Cross of Christ at the time when she was made a soldier of Christ, gave a gift that was a symbol of a far higher reality than any degree of local respect and veneration.

Behind the hand that gave her that precious Relic, which, characteristically, she gave immediately to the Church, another Hand was holding a cross in the shadow of the years to come, a cross that would measure itself to the white depths of heroism. God chose Julie Billiart, and when God chooses, it is not with the beckoning of a finger, but with the steady in-pressing of a two-edged sword which seeks the nerve and sinew, the bone and the marrow, in order that, through suffering, it may reveal what grace can accomplish in the weakness of human nature. Only thus can He fashion souls to stand forth, with the sublime cry: "Be ye followers of me as I am of Christ." Julie Billiart stands at the head of a great religious movement, and it is of the economy of salvation that her soul should be a mighty one, formed and made deep with suffering. When God chooses a soul for a God-like vocation, He puts His Hand on the loom, busily weaving the mediocre patterns of mediocre lives, and, where in the great tapestry of His Providence He designs a pattern for that chosen soul, He threads the loom with the pain of life. . . .

In the rhythm of Cuvilly, as slow and as quiet as the movement of the heavy soil lifting and sliding under the plough, Julie Billiart reached her sixteenth year. Life moved quietly in the home of the Billiarts, with its round of household tasks, gardens to be tended, fowl to be fed, and prayer in the dawn and in the lengthening shadows, linking, vivifying, giving a meaning to it all. The little drapery store was doing well: the land was good: the name Billiart was spoken with respect. But . . . "Doth Job fear God for naught? . . . Put forth thy hand and touch all that he hath . . . skin for skin, yea . . . put forth thy hand now and touch his bone and his flesh." When Julie Billiart reached her sixteenth year, the hand of God was already stretched forth towards her and her family—the hand that chastises where it loves.

A gaping door, a broken window, some fabrics lying in the dust: such was the sorry sight that met Jean-François Billiart one morning as he came to open his little store. It is hard on a man when he has laboured to build his little world and wakes to find it in fragments about his feet. Jean-François stooped and picked up what the thieves had dropped in their scramble: yet it seemed a deliberate mockery, for he found that little else remained on the shelves inside. He knew the value of the stock that had been stolen and he knew that its loss meant bankruptcy. Sorrowfully, he gathered into a couple of bundles the little stock that remained, left the door swinging behind him in a gesture of futility, and went home. Later in the day, some friends brought him a few pieces of linen and expensive lace which the thieves, alarmed perhaps by some noise, had dropped into a disused well. Perhaps their very whiteness was

a source of danger. They were not white now, but
muddy, heavy, torn. Jean-François lifted them one by
one, and one by one he let them drop on the floor of
the little kitchen. They fell clumsily in an unlovely
heap. Useless. Futile. Even the land must go now.
Suddenly very weary, he sat down and buried his head
in his hands.

When Jean-François Billiart stooped, to grope dis-
consolately among the fragments of his dreams, he
found that a child's hand—the hand of his daughter—
had reached the wreckage before him : a hand in which
there was freshness and strength, bringing hope with
it and forward-looking thoughts : a hand that reached
out to him with something of that mysterious power
which the Sacred Writer celebrated in the words : " A
little child shall lead them." For as he sat that morning with the wet, clinging garment of his desolation
about him, he felt two warm and firm hands grasping
his hands, and as it were a sudden gentle breathing of
a warm wind in the cold, stony places of his heart. He
looked up, and saw Julie's eyes on him, with compassion
and understanding in their depths. The shadow of the
cross was to deepen on the path of Jean-François, for
this was but the beginning of sorrows : but the eyes
of his child, shining where that shadow was deepest,
would teach him to be resigned.

There is no realism like the realism of the saints.
They are not ethereal beings, beating luminous wings
in a kind of spiritual garden hung between heaven and
earth, but men and women who came to grips with the
hard, unlovely things of life, and made of them a
beauty that is the wonder of angels : for not to angels
was it said—" Take up your cross "—but to us. It cannot be too often emphasized : our holiness must be
taken from the heights, with pain, and the saint is he
who has realistically accepted the pain of life, and by
it has scaled the heights, to stand, larger than human,

JULIE BILLIART SPEAKS OF GOD TO THE HARVESTERS

JULIE RODE MORE THAN TWENTY MILES TO BEAUVAIS

against the sky, clothed with the seamless garment he has woven, with Grace, from the agony of his soul. With magnificent audacity, St. Paul has called on us to "fill up what is wanting to the sufferings of Christ": a text whose meaning holds one of the great secrets at the heart of Christianity. . . . And so it was that the hands which warmed the cold hands of François Billiart and the eyes which rested on his like a caress, were the hands and the eyes of a spiritual realist. For, very shortly after this, Julie Billiart had taken her place among the hardest workers in the harvest fields, that she might save her parents from utter ruin. There was a strength and a determination in her attitude, far beyond her years—a strength drawn from that prayer-filled silence of dawn, when her soul fed on the Bread of the strong, and heaven lay about her in the noiseless manna-falling of Eucharistic blessings.

"There is a beautiful consistency in Blessed Julie's char-acter," writes one of her biographers, "and a unity in her life which cannot fail to strike the careful reader: its large and simple lines run through her entire career. To her apostolic soul the fields were verily white unto harvest; and at midday, when the reapers rested, she would sit in their midst and teach them to sing hymns, or read aloud to them some pious book which, at once, instructed and interested them. And so great was the young girl's influence over these rough labourers, that they wished for no other amusement when they could have Julie with her book, or still more captivating conversation. They even petitioned her to assemble them on Sunday also; but on that day she gave herself entirely to God and to her family."

What remained of the stock in the little shop had also to be sold, and it is easy to bargain with a man who is reeling from a blow, so that the little stock was chang-ing hands at a tenth of its value. Again, Julie took charge of the situation in no uncertain fashion. She saddled a horse, rode more than twenty miles to Beauvais, a town in which she knew no one, and entered

C

the first shop she saw open.   The firmness and decision in her action were born of prayerful trust in God, and that trust was rewarded, for the owner of the shop was an honest and sympathetic tradesman who listened to her story and paid her the proper price for her bundle. This was but one of the many occasions when this girl took a grip on the hard realities of life, with the cool, firm grasp of a spiritual realist.

All these external activities were veined with works of pure charity; visiting the sick, attending to the poor, working for the Church, and their breath was prayer. We have already noticed her skill in Church embroidery, and it is inspiring to see how this was the occasion of one of those touches of what might be called the courtesy of God.   In His designs, this girl was on the threshold of a cross-filled life—first, as one flung down by God and afflicted; then, raised up to a life of intense apostolic activity, never unshadowed by the cross.   It was splendidly fitting, therefore, that He should have allowed her soul to know the deep, prayer-laden silence that is the heart of the contemplative life, a silence that, in the fulness of time, must be the necessary heart of her own active life, sending great, calm pulsations of spiritual energy through all the heaped-up cares, anxieties, misunderstandings and crosses of the Apostolate.   "Her skill in church embroidery," the biographer we have cited writes, "took her from time to time to the Carmelite Convent of Compiègne, renowned at that time throughout all the countryside for its strict observance and the holy lives of its inmates." There were sixteen Sisters in this Convent, and some years later, in 1793, during the Reign of Terror, these intrepid souls were to leave the Conciergerie, chanting the *Salve Regina* as they walked calmly and recollectedly to the guillotine. . . . There are great moments of silence in every man's life to which he owes all that is finest in him.   When God calls a soul to a high perfec-

tion, He first plunges it into a silence wherein the voice
of the world dies to a faint whisper which cannot hinder
the intimacies of God.   In silence of soul, the great,
simple lines of spirituality are laid down.   There must
have been a very special quality about the silence and
the spiritual conversation of Carmelite Compiègne,
for it was the seeding place of martyrs.   Such a quality
must have been immediately appealing to a spiritual
soul like that of Julie Billiart.   It was indeed fitting
that her soul should have known a few moments of that
God-filled silence, that, in its strength, she might walk
the rough and flint-strewn ways which God lays down
before the feet of His saints.

 To feel that our hands are gripping and steadying
the shaking world of those we love is one of the purest
satisfactions life can give.   Julie Billiart knew that
satisfaction, but it was too human an emotion in a soul
that God was shaping to great things.   It is characteristic
of the curve of God's dealings with men, that those on
whom He sets His especial seal should first be struck
down in utter impotence, so that, by human standards,
they may be reckoned among the lives broken and made
useless by misfortune.   God shapes His wonders with
apparently blunted tools, which seem only to hack and
rough-hew, yet, to heavenly eyes, they shape beauty
that is the joy of angels.   God was thus to shape the life
of Julie Billiart under hard blows of blunted tools,
blunt as the nails of Calvary.   A poet has compared the
years to the passing feet of great black oxen, pounding
things to dust.   God seems sometimes to pound a life
mercilessly to dust, with cross upon heavy cross: but
the dust is precious, far above the proud bricks and
mortar of human judgment and human planning,
because of that dust God makes His spiritual world.
" Unless the seed falling into the ground dies," Christ
said, using another metaphor, "itself remaineth alone:
but if it dies, it bringeth forth fruit a hundredfold."

The winter of 1774 saw a great change in the once robust health of Julie Billiart. She had been under-fed and over-worked; she had known cares and anxieties beyond her years: her sight was threatened. The whole family made a pilgrimage to Montreuil to venerate an image of the Holy Face, and their faith and devotion obtained the complete restoration of her sight. But something more precious than bodily sight was given to Julie Billiart, for she had learned to see the Hand of God in the sufferings of her life, and to bless that Hand whose chastisement she saw as the shadow of a divine caress. God accepted the loving resignation of His servant, and, to reward her in heaven's mysterious coinage, He reached into the darkness to where the crosses are kept for saints. In 1774, an event occurred which was to change the course of life for Julie Billiart.

Every city, every town, every village is a criss-cross of human moods and motives: and therefore, we can scarcely guess at the amalgam of petty jealousy, of resentment, perhaps of politics, that led to a few moments of melodrama in the usually placid kitchen of the Billiarts. It was silent one winter's evening, as darkness settled, gathering things more closely about the little farm-house and intensifying the peace and cosiness within. Suddenly there was a sound of splinter-ing glass, and a great stone landed in the centre of the kitchen. Immediately after, a pistol was fired at Jean-François Billiart, but it missed its mark and, apart from the fright and consternation it caused, all seemed well. Yet, it only seemed so: for that stone and that pistol shattered the nervous system of Julie Billiart, so that their effect on her could be symbolized by that broken window and that shower of splintered glass. An inadequate symbol. The following morning, Jean-François would have put another pane of glass in the window, and the splintered glass would have been swept away out of their mind: but that other shattering was the beginning of thirty years' suffering for this devoted daughter. Soon she was being tortured in all her limbs as though the marrow of her bones had been changed to a kind of liquid pain, so that this once very active girl had perforce to drag herself from room to room. Yet even intense pain could not turn her from charity, and therefore many a soul was helped into eternity by Julie who had come to the bedside of the dying through a river of pain.

In all this charity there was still the consolation of giving: and now this, too, was asked of her. In the eighteenth century, the panacea for all ills was to bleed the patient. Julie was subjected to this late in 1782, and as a result she became a complete cripple. Gone were the chances of paying her daily calls to her Eucharistic Lord: gone were the chances of serving the neighbour: gone were her dreams.

Or were they?

The cross was a heavy one. Losses and physical sufferings may be great: but more searing still is the pain of a sensitive soul which sees itself powerless to serve the urgent needs of those it loves. This was the cross that was now laid on Julie Billiart. Yet we may be sure that one whose whole emphasis in later spiritual teaching was to be on faith, who was to write to her future co-Foundress, "This is the grace I beg the good God to bestow on you that you may advance daily in this holy exercise of faith, for thus it is that God fashions His saints"; one whose very soul-fibre was simplicity, "since," as she said, "the spirit of God is the spirit of simplicity"; one whose years were to echo with the cry—"Oh, how good is the good God"—we may be sure that such a soul received with divinely inspired equanimity, the apparent lifting from her life of life's last consolation, the ability of a broken life to serve the broken. We have no letter of hers from this period of her life, but the sentiments she expressed in a letter of September 1st, 1795, to her future co-Foundress are surely a mirror of those earlier years. She writes:

" Since the spirit of God is the spirit of simplicity, the surest way for us is to keep ourselves in that attitude of mind which approximates to the simplicity of faith, avoiding above all things all reasonings which lead to anxiety of mind, and would cause us to lose peace of soul, our one great treasure."

A biographer's task is to present the life of Blessed Julie Billiart so that these words are written large on every page. For faith and simplicity, and the simplicity of faith mirroring the simplicity of God, are the glowing secrets at its heart.

Again, let us illustrate from a letter of 1795, and see the sentiments in it as but the mellowing of what was already in her soul during those early years of suffering:

" You wish me to speak of my wretched body. It is not worth the trouble, but since you wish it, I will tell you that it is worth nothing, nothing at all. My days, thanks be to God, are full of suffering, and my nights are sometimes worse. But, my dear good friend, what are my sufferings compared with the love God has for me? Yes, I confess I am indeed happy when the good God gives me the grace to suffer much. Then I give a little share to all my good friends in the Faith, through the infinite merits of our good Saviour."

Thus does she make light of hours that dragged their slow pain across the weary wastes of her days and her nights. In that pain, her gift of prayer was born, and of that prayer were born the mighty things of her life. "You know also," she was to write, "that the path of prayer is the path of death to self." The winepress of her sufferings gave the rich red wine of her prayer, and there were no dregs of self to cloud that wine. Of the heights of prayer to which she attained at this time, P. Sellier wrote:

" What struck me most in Mère Julie, was a quite uncommon

gift of prayer, and I believe she was raised to a very high degree of contemplation. She spent in this holy exercise, four or five hours a day. At such times she was to be seen perfectly rapt in God, motionless, all use of her senses suspended, and her countenance glowing with heavenly sweetness. The noises made around her were powerless to distract her during these divine communications. She came to herself from this mysterious state with a visible effort, and only after someone had gently shaken her or pulled her by the arm. I am speaking of the time when she lay paralysed upon a bed of pain."

Every day Monsieur l'Abbé Dangicourt brought to her her Lord in the Blessed Sacrament. Her every day was a rack of pain: but it was manna-white with Eucharistic beauty, and in that manna she found heroic strength.

We began this chapter by saying that the Incarnation has its full meaning in that it is the way to final transfiguration and deification: that God became man that man might become as God. There is no more powerful means of bringing about this happy consummation than the Holy Eucharist. In a magnificent phrase from one of her letters, Blessed Julie expresses this deification of man, and at the same time reveals her own tremendous, living grasp of a living truth:

"A soul that has the happiness of possessing her God in the august Sacrament of His love, is worthy of the adoration of angels and men."

Faith. Simplicity. And the purity of vision that is the marriage of both.

CHAPTER THREE

THE DREGS OF THE CHALICE

IN Book Two of his famous work, Carlyle has this comment to make on the religious face of France in 1789: "For granting even that Religion were dead; that it had died, half-centuries ago, with unutterable Dubois; or emigrated lately to Alsace, with Necklace-Cardinal Rohan; or that it now walked as goblin *revenant*, with Bishop Talleyrand of Autun; yet does not the Shadow of Religion, the Cant of Religion, still linger?"

It is easy to point to the Dubois, the Rohans, the Talleyrands in every age of the Church, and to regard religion as the odour of an empty vase which once brimmed with the rich, spiritual spices of Christianity. But this is to limit one's vision to the tangled briars of history, and leave unnoticed the priceless violets in the undergrowth. There is no mention of Julie Billiart in any page of Carlyle. We hear of the iniquities of Dubois; of the wily twistings of Talleyrand, "that irreverend Reverence of Autun"; of the Cardinal de Rohan, in whose hands history has placed a lady's necklace where Beads of prayer should be—of all of these we hear in the great Mississippi rush of rhetoric that is Carlyle's prose, but not a word of her whose strength was her silent suffering, and whose achievement would remain, a living, vital, pulsating achievement in the world to-day, when all these have become remote and spectre-like in the mist of dissolution which marks the path of time. It is indeed an arresting thought, that when the last thread is woven, and God turns the great tapestry of life that men may see His view of it, the world will look in vain for the emblazoned deeds of its heroes, and those heroes themselves, seeing the apotheosis of all they had proudly despised, will find those words of Scripture on their lips: "We fools esteemed their life madness and their end without honour: behold how they are numbered among the children of God and their lot is with the saints." For it is the apparently formless mass of knots at the back of earth's tapestry that has significance for God, so that, in the end, in the sounding of a trumpet, the dark and obscure and "meaningless" things of life: the formless mass of knots, will reveal an eternal Design worthy of God, the beauty of which will gather up all creation's praise of its Creator, and justify the mysterious ways of God to men.

In the great rush and roar of revolutionary France, it would be difficult for worldly wisdom to find a life with as little apparent significance for her own or for any other age, as that of Julie Billiart. Flung down like something useless, paralysed even while her body was racked with convulsive suffering, she lay on her bed of pain, and there was no hint of greatness for the worldly wise in the poverty of that little room, in the brick floor, in the little window through which the ochre of twilight would seep to mellow all the things about her, but powerless to soften the grip of her pain. But there were other features of this room that would have had significance for the angels: there was a crucifix, a crucifix with a living context, a crucifix that was the symbol of a cross formed and fashioned of a woman's suffering: there was also a catechism in that shaking hand laid on the counterpane: round that cross and that catechism the plans of God were already forming. For the children would gather around her bed and she would explain the catechism to them, and because she herself had penetrated to the fountain-source of Christianity—the *fons saliens*—her words were like spring water, limpid, fresh, with no hint of staleness. Already in that little room, and in that little scene, the great Institute of Notre Dame existed fully in germ: all its significance is there, and when the followers of Julie Billiart would renew themselves, it is here they must in spirit return.

We are told that Julie's " tenderest zeal was lavished on the children preparing for their First Communion ": many years later, the Abbé Trouvelot of Cuvilly tells of old people who said to him as he was about to administer Holy Viaticum: " Wait a bit, Monsieur le Curé; I must first say the Acts which Julie Billiart taught me." Even so can a seed of prayer be placed in the dewy freshness of a child's soul, and be found blossoming in an old man's prayer, when the shadows of the grave are about him, and the Food for the journey is at hand. Let such a consideration be the solace and reward of those who labour, through many dry and tiresome hours, to instruct many unto justice, " Wait a bit, Monsieur le Curé " . . . if an Archangel could be jealous it would be at praise like that!

" Other visitors, too," her biographer tells us, " pressed into the poor little room: great ladies from Paris, whom the summer brought down to their châteaux round about Cuvilly, Madame de Pont-l'Abbé from her seat at Gournay-sur-Aronde, the pious Madame de Séchelles, who venerated Julie both as a Saint and a living image of Christ Crucified, and the Countess Baudoin with her three bright girls." We shall meet these names again—especially that of the Countess Baudoin, the " bonne dame " of Julie's letters: while " the three bright girls " are part of the first grouping in the early years. These good ladies became constant visitors to the saintly invalid, and because of the inconvenience they caused by passing through the kitchen —for a kitchen is a woman's workshop—they had a

special door made from the outside into her room, and
they replaced its cold brick floor by one of oak boards.
But their place in this history is more than that of
casual comforters of a sick girl.   In the designs of God
they were to be instrumental in bringing to Julie
Billiart the priceless boon of a twin-soul, whose vision
would fuse glowingly with hers.   But they suspected
nothing of this.   They saw a poor invalid and their pity
was awakened: they grasped something of Julie's deep
holiness and because it was Christ-warm in a cold world,
they brought their lives close to the flame.   In this
sequestered way of silent suffering and deep prayer, the
year 1789 dawned for Julie Billiart, and seemed as
though its rhythm would be as motionless as that of all
the years that had gone before.

But, in Paris, there were blood-filled clouds in the
dawn of 1789—clouds that would move across the sky,
until France, the land of St. Louis, the Eldest Daughter
of the Church, would wade in her own best blood; and
the guillotine would stand, corpse-gaunt, like a cynical
leer: almost like the cynical leer on the old, withered
face of Monsieur François de Voltaire (a face like dried
and crumpled paper), the man who had seen it all, had
worked towards it, and who, ten years before, had
boasted in death-bed cynicism that to the end he had
danced on the edge of his tomb.   Aristocratic France,
too, had danced through the brilliant surface of a world
that bubbled like champagne, wit and wine and beautiful women its soul; a world with a laugh and a sophis-
ticated sneer in its heart for all that was holy, because
holiness, as Madame de Chautard said, in one of her
brilliant after-dinner moments, was so utterly naïve: a
world, then, that had danced and danced, and was still
sniggering at its own witty sallies, even when the
first drops of warning blood had splashed about the
feet of the dancers.   The dance was soon to become a
dance of death; the society snigger was to lose its

silvered nuance of suggestiveness, as the great subject of
wit became My Lady Guillotine's fastidious taste in
blood; and the laugh was riotously on other lips, the
lips of those who had been just part of the scurrying
dust of carriage wheels, or merely outcrops of the soil
they tilled.   There was mob-hysteria in the laugh, and
nothing was sacred to it.   There was a rush to make all
things new: the past was ashes to be flung in the face
of God, for the rubble was of His making, and even He
was to be put wise to the error of His ways, by an
omniscient and triumphant People, in order that He
might take His place in a brave new world.

A new world would have a new Church, a Church of
the People and from the People.   In July of the following year—1790—the National Assembly, the People's
Parliament, voted the Civil Constitution of the Clergy,
an Act that would make of the priesthood of France a
puppet-show on state-controlled strings: "*vox populi,*"
as expressed through the laws and ordinances of the
realm, being indeed "*vox Dei,*" with prison and the
guillotine as its sanction.   Some among the spiritual
cedars of Lebanon, long sapless and riddled with the dry
rot of worldliness, fell before the first onslaught of
secularization.   But they were few compared with the
number of those who stood firm by reason of the
mysterious strength of prayer that was in them: priests
like the Abbé de la Marche who stood at the foot of
the scaffold and secretly blessed each of the Carmelite
Sisters of Compiègne as she mounted to the guillotine;
or the Curé of Cuvilly who hid like a hunted animal, in
a dark hole behind a hen-house, that he might creep
out at night and bring spiritual comfort to his flock.
For six months this good priest spent his days hiding
in the earth.   They ferreted him out and he had to
flee.   Finally, in the shadow of the celebrated Calvary
of Mont-Valérien in Paris, still faithful, still secretly
ministering, he went to his reward.   There was much in

those last months of his life to make weary the soul of
the Pastor of Cuvilly: but is it fanciful to think that,
crouched in the earth-hole or hunted from place to
place, he found prayerful comfort in the thought that
France, for all her stupid waywardness, could still
produce a soul like that of Julie Billiart.   Turning
to her letters, we find that characteristic of all the
saints—a lifting of the eyes to the eternal hills, a
pressing forward that has an urgency and a thirst
in it:

"My daughter, I will leave them the earth in exchange for
heaven as soon as they like. I am not much troubled about
it. We shall go away, my daughter, you and I, we shall go
away together. We shall leave them on earth with all their
estates and houses; we shall press on to the house of our Father
in our heavenly Fatherland."

Little wonder if, with a spirit like this in its midst,
the district in which she lived was found to have stood
firm in the storm, a fact which Monsieur d'Héry had
no hesitation in attributing to the "happy influence"
of Julie Billiart. She was one of those who think in
straight lines, and there are straight, unwavering lines
in her attitude towards the Constitutional Clergy, as
can be seen from the following extract from a letter of
November 15th, 1795:

"I congratulate you, my dear good friend, that the good God
gives you the opportunity of being useful to souls; but walk
with caution, for present circumstances make this work difficult
for you. You say it seems to you it would be better to be
schismatic rather than to be utterly without religion. But, my
dear friend, you cannot have weighed the matter, for we must
not, in conscience, leave our brethren in error. If they go
to the instructions of an intruder, they are *ipso facto* out of
the way of salvation. . . . All those good folk, who find it
utterly impossible to get into touch with their legitimate
pastors, will not be punished for that, and it is better for them
to remain all their lives without instruction, without Mass.

The good God . . . will send an angel from heaven to them rather than allow them to perish for ever."

The uncompromising attitude which this extract indicates, met the intruder who usurped the place of Monsieur l'Abbé in Cuvilly. The unfortunate hireling attempted to minister the consolations of religion to Cuvilly's "saint." He was firmly and courteously stopped on the threshold of the little room and turned away. The Church of Christ in every age is saved by those who will not bow the knee to schism, even when schism comes dressed in all the robes of Christ's priesthood and claiming to carry Christ. Life held nothing for Julie Billiart except in so far as its every detail, its every tone, its every ideal could be grouped about the Blessed Eucharist, and find there eternal significance. Now this great, living centre was removed from the days of Julie Billiart, and it pleased God that the shadows should gather and darken her soul.

Julie's whole attitude drew on her the wrath of the Revolution. She was a harbourer, they said, of clerical traitors to the People: "La Dévote" had betrayed them. There was an angry muttering in the air about her. Madame de Pont-l'Abbé had grave fears for her friend's safety. She came in her carriage and removed Julie to her own château of Gournay-sur-Aronde. With Julie went her niece, Felicity, a girl of sixteen. It is hard to fix the lines of Felicity's character: an affectionate child-type, perhaps, who, though she devoted herself to Julie through a difficult time and even showed resourcefulness, remained fundamentally dependent on Julie and in need of her. She had come to Julie at the age of seven, and had refused to leave her. Julie deeply appreciated her devotion, but that did not prevent her from weighing her niece in the spiritual scales by which she judged everything and everybody. "I am very pleased," she writes in January 1796, "with my poor little Felicity: she would like very much to improve, she works at it a little, she has a little more simplicity." When Felicity is mentioned in the letters, it is as the Martha of the early years: she knew the rôle of Martha, but there is a suggestion that her aunt would have liked to discover a little more of Mary in her, too.

The guillotine, however, soon shadowed the household of Gournay, and as a result, Madame de Pont-l'Abbé fled into exile, leaving her invalid friend in the care of a dependant. Soon, too, the hue and cry caught up with Julie, an angry crowd surged about the house, and fierce cries—the cry revolutionary France knew so well, a cry with hysterical blood-lust in it—struck terror into the household. The mob had torn down the village Calvary and had splintered it to make a pile "whereon they intended to burn, at one and the same time, the image of their Redeemer and the frail body of His suffering disciple." There were a few moments of feverish activity within the house. There were sounds of splintering wood, of a gate slivered under battering-rams, and the yells for "La Dévote" were already filling the inner courtyard, as they rushed the poor invalid into a side lane, laid her with more haste than care in an open country cart, and covered her with straw. A minute later the mob was rushing madly through the house. The ugliness of their mood is shown in a phrase from the Memoirs of the co-Foundress, in which she tells us that they intended first of all to drag her from her bed of suffering "and make her dance on the counterpane." This is the mood of the purple garment and the reed placed in the right hand: and when men make a mockery of pain, then indeed the animal in them has bared its claws and its fangs. We are told that the Concierge met the rioters so bravely, and upbraided them so roundly, that they desisted from their purpose and went away.

Meantime, every nerve on fire with pain and half-smothered with the straw, Julie lay listening to the cursing and blasphemy of the mob. Yet, as she confided later, there was no fear of death in her soul, for she would have rejoiced had it pleased God that she should suffer and die for Christ on a splintered Calvary. Her only sorrow, she said, was the knowledge that not even the revealing of her hiding-place could stop that flow of blasphemy.

It was getting dark and the mood of a mob is never to be trusted. The Concierge explained to Julie that she must be got away immediately to Compiègne, and that her journey would have to be made in that farm-cart where she could be hidden under the straw. Her niece, Felicity, climbed into the cart with her, and the servants started on the journey. It was an unsprung cart and the roads were bad. Every part of her body was racked with excruciating pain. For safety, they were obliged to take long and devious back-roads, for the hunt after Julie had begun again. There were moments of alarm and anxiety, when as the early Memoirs of the Institute relate, "she passed through a mob of revolutionaries who were searching for her and who unwittingly allowed their prey to escape, because whom God protects is well protected." Night had fallen, a long winter night stiff with frost, when they drew into the courtyard of an inn. Quickly they removed the straw from her, and then, in sudden terror for their own safety, they all fled. Paralysed, frozen with cold, a heavy, dull throb of pain in nerve, in bone, in sinew, in flesh, she lay helpless through the long night. Felicity found it very difficult to get her to take a little wine. Dawn came with the slowness of pain, and with it came help. Two pious ladies named Chambon, took her into their house and took care of her. But the search was closing in around her, and it soon became dangerous to stay longer in that house.

HER JOURNEY WOULD HAVE TO BE MADE IN THE
FARM CART

Holiness was one of the few crimes left in revolutionary France, and as a criminal she was hunted from house to house. Five times during the three or four years she remained at Compiègne she was obliged to change her place of hiding. The prayer that was constantly on her lips in these years has been handed down to us. It is the homesick prayer of the homeless—the homeless whose home, in Francis Thompson's beautiful phrase, must needs "be all of sky"; "Lord, wilt Thou not lodge me in Paradise, since I can no longer find shelter on earth?" Her mind is mirrored in some words she used in those years: "How happy should we be to resemble our good Master who had not whereon to lay His head: We are surrounded by the dead and the dying: let us then pray to die to all by universal detachment."

In June 1792 she had received news of the death of her father. Life had been hard on Jean-François Billiart, but when he crossed its threshold and stood before God, he must have been consoled to see that his trials, his crosses, his disappointments had a double significance. They were the shaping of his own soul to God's thought for him: and they were the shadows cast by crosses measured to his daughter's magnificent heroism.

Those years in Compiègne had played havoc with the health of Julie Billiart. She was a nervous wreck, her jaws were contracted so that she could make a pitiful attempt at saying a word only after the most violent efforts. She very soon had to content herself with a language of signs. Physical suffering had been racking the body of Julie Billiart for twenty years: now, at the age of forty-one, she had reached the last stage of helplessness, and even then the searing, searching, two-edged sword of God's election had not finished its work of preparation in the soul of this heroic woman. For God wills that His own awful cry—"My God, My God, why hast Thou forsaken me?"—should have an echo in the

D

souls of His chosen ones, in order that they should be purified by the deepest of all agony—the agony of the apparent withdrawal of God from a soul that thirsts for Him alone.

This apparent withdrawal of God takes the form of a complete loss of all sensible comfort in prayer or good works, leaving an aridity which warps and dries up the soul. Prayer seems a white, gritty dust on tongue and throat, there is no freshness in it: this drying, chapping east wind of the soul came to Julie Billiart at a time when her vitality was at its lowest. It was the last touch of God's long preparing: a soul stood before Him helpless, groping in its own darkness: strong only in its unwavering trust in Him. Looking on that soul, He loved it, for the imprint of the crucifying nails was there. He saw His work that He had wrought through human pain, and He knew that it was good. The spirit in which Julie accepted such trials is evident from a beautiful passage in one of her letters:

"However severe His guidance may appear to us at times, it is always the guidance of a Father Who is infinitely good, wise and kind, Who leads us to our goal by different paths. And after all, my dear good friend, let us be honest—Is it not true that we tend to spoil the work of grace in us? Hence it is to our advantage to experience the withdrawal of this same grace, and abandonment by God. Then we must act as little children do in the dark—clasp the hand of father or mother and go where we are led."

It was because Julie Billiart knew how to live that last sentence that she stood before God as a perfect instrument for His designs.

What those designs were, He now unequivocally revealed to her. One day her prayer changed to vision, in which she beheld the hill of Calvary with her crucified Lord surrounded by a multitude of virgins wearing a religious habit she had never seen before. The faces of the virgins were so distinctly present to her that she was able later to recognize them when they came to join her. "God wills that you should enter our society," she said to Françoise Blin de Bourdon, "for I saw you among ours at Compiègne." The face of Françoise must indeed have been very clear in the vision, for she was to be essential to the realization of a mighty design. We must now focus attention on Françoise: for it would be impossible to treat adequately of Blessed Julie Billiart without doing justice to her twin-soul, Françoise Blin de Bourdon. As well present Clare without Francis, Jane Chantal without Francis de Sales, Aquinas without Bonaventure, Ausonius without Paulinus. These soul friendships are intense and vivid unions of spirit with spirit, and are earth's reflection of angelic union. Their symbol is the mystical flame which enveloped the Portiuncula, when Francis broke bread with Clare. The occasion of Julie's meeting with Françoise arose from an invitation sent to Julie by the Countess Baudoin, whom we have met at the invalid's bedside in Cuvilly, to join her in Amiens. There was a prophecy of persecution in the vision given to Julie, and therefore, we are told, "she felt within herself the strongest possible repugnance to set her face towards the city which was to be for her the scene of the persecution she had beheld." However, she came finally to consider the invitation as a sign of God's Will. A comfortable carriage was sent to Compiègne, and once more Julie and Felicity set off together.

She left Compiègne with the vision fresh in her soul. It was as if slowly she had mounted her Calvary, and had met Christ there. He had spoken to her from the Cross, telling her that with the living, virginal temples of the Holy Spirit standing about Him, she was to make a thing of beauty for God, for angels and for men. He sealed the vision with a promise, the strange, loving promise of God. Julie heard the words spoken plainly as she wondered what the vision could mean:

"Behold the spiritual daughters whom I give you in the Institute which I promise to mark with My Cross."

As strength and consolation, God was soon to give her a friend. Her features were very clear to Julie in the vision. Perhaps she stood nearest the Cross, and her face had a greater radiance.

CHAPTER FOUR

THE OTHER CORNER-STONE

THERE is no such thing in the world as chance. Two chosen lives cross each other, and their place of meeting is a luminous point in the plan of God. To human eyes, there may be an element of incongruity in such meeting. The lives may be socially poles apart, in the contrast of cottage and castle: but at the point of meeting, the narrow limits of both castle and cottage retreat before the greater significance of Grace, just as the mean walls of the inn at Emmaus faded for the Disciples into a God-swept horizon when they watched two beautiful hands breaking bread. Grace is a mighty leveller, and there is no equality like the divine equality among men who kneel to receive their Eucharistic Lord: "For each, the entire monopoly of Day—for each, the whole of the devoted Sun." This is the climate of the Commandment that is like unto the First. Grace takes the soul like a zephyr coming from the eternal hills of God: the soul that breathes it deeply knows no barriers of rank or station, and the castle bends to the cottage that the cottage may sanctify it.

Such a soul was Madame de Fouquesolles, Viscoun- tess of Doullens, who was no impertinent patronizer mixing social snobbery with her largesse, but one whose charity had a kneeling humility in it. Often, as she left the château of Gézaincourt to visit the people of her estate, a little girl, with a light step and a silvery laugh, skipped along at her side. This was her grand-daughter, Marie-Louise-Françoise Blin de Bourdon, Demoiselle de Gézaincourt, whose life was to find full significance in the apparently trivial fact that it crossed the life of a peasant woman of Cuvilly. But in that crossing, there was a mighty fusion of soul with soul, and of the fusion was born a glory to the Church of God—the Institute of the Sisters of Notre Dame.

The childhood of Julie Billiart and the childhood of Françoise Blin de Bourdon present a great contrast, for the one has a texture of rough homespun and other other the smoothness of velvet. There were many elements of poetry in the surroundings of Françoise—the poetry of north-east Picardy, of woods that continue the forest of the Ardennes, of deep, winding lanes drowsy with hawthorn and cooled by ash and alder, and added to all this, the graciousness of an aristocratic home. With a turn of phrase reminiscent of the Romantic poets of Julie's time, her French biographer speaks of her soul as "a sensitive lyre, ever ready to vibrate in unison with nature, that, with nature's sweet harmonies, it might hymn the power and the beauty of the Creator." And again—"Her response to flowers and verdure, to birds and butterflies, to play of sunlight and shade, was both delicate and deep." By contrast, such poetic response to created beauty in the soul of Julie Billiart had early been transformed into passionate love of its Creator and, on the human plane, reality had come all too soon, to harden the lines of life for her, and there was little poetry in the long journeys with merchandise or the hot hours of the harvest fields.

Françoise was the third and youngest child of Pierre Louis de Blin, Viscount of Domart-en-Ponthieu and Marie-Louise-Claudine, daughter of the Baron de Fouquesolles, Viscount de Doullens. Her grandmother and sponsor, Madame de Fouquesolles, became so attached to the child that she could not bear to part from her, and therefore it was agreed that she should be brought up at Gézaincourt. Every element was present, then, for the growth of just another of those petulant, passionate, vain and empty ladies who flourished like lusciously perfumed weeds in the social and political soil of eighteenth-century France. This was the age when the lady's fan and the statesman's quill lay side by side on the desk of state, and decisions were more often a matter of the fan than of the quill. There are indications, indeed, that Françoise might have been drawn into the perfumed swirl, but for the sanctified commonsense of her grandmother, because the child soon began to show signs of being a very self-willed little lady. Self-willed, yes; but self-willed with a difference. Listen to her biographer:

"Her grandmother had given her a pair of shoes ornamented with the large rosettes of the period, and the child spoilt them by running near the lake in the park. When Mlle. Ursule, the governess, was lamenting over the fallen splendour of the rosettes, and reproving the little girl, Françoise answered: 'It is no sin to spoil rosettes, so why should you care about it?' . . . Another day she was stung by a wasp and screamed aloud with pain, whereupon Mlle. Ursule told her that she had much better be quiet and suffer the pain for her sins. 'I have not committed any sins yet,' was the quick reply, 'but,' drying her tears, 'I will stop crying for the love of Jesus.'"

So deep and effective were the teaching and example of Madame de Fouquesolles that the child was unconsciously measuring things by an ultimate standard, and seeing them *sub specie aeternitatis*. Indeed, the only way to control her rich, wilful nature was to appeal to such ultimates. Her grandmother would counter her moods, not with scoldings or punishments, but with an appeal to the example of the Christ-Child: and then, Françoise would immediately obey, even inflicting pain on herself in atonement. A wise guide countered her wilfulness by a finger pointed to the Will of God, and thus, even in the correction of her faults, the child's whole life was orientated towards God.

Searching for glimpses of the halo over the cot is

often mere wishful thinking: yet it is true that certain childish sayings and doings have a significant place in the finished portrait. There is, for instance, the saying recorded from Françoise after her first confession. Her governess explained that the Precious Blood applied in the Sacrament satisfied abundantly for her sins. "Then let me go again," she answered, "only what can one say the second time?" This question indicates the simplicity and sincerity which were hers in such a high degree when the years had brought their fulness. Meantime, her comment on the penance she received—two *Paters*—at her first Confession, shows that she was a perfectly natural child and not a pious precocity. She remarks that her grandmother would have given her more.

With the coming of summer, society used to descend on the quiet of Gézaincourt. Elegant lords and ladies surrounded the little girl, petted her, teased her into quick and amusing repartee and laughed at her wit. Madame de Fouquesolles was quick to see the danger in this, and therefore she arranged to have her accepted as a pupil in the Benedictine Convent at Doullens during each of the visiting seasons. The rigid lines of Port-Royal are clearly discernible in the educational ideas of Doullens: there was no thought of amusing the child, no learn-as-you-play methods, but solid exercises designed to form the judgment and train the will. One of the pupils who later became a follower of Julie Billiart has summed up her impression of life in Benedictine Saint-Michel at Doullens thus: "It seemed as though our teachers foresaw the awful Revolution, and knew their vocation as, above all, the preparation of women with the stamina to stand firm. We had little of the frivolities of life: holidays were rare, and there was a consistent seriousness of purpose in our lives which conduced to a habit of reflection." . . . The atmosphere of Saint-Michel was good for Françoise. In it she felt the first stirring of a definite desire to reach out towards bigger things. Through it, she was to receive the strength to carry herself bravely through the dark days of the Revolution.

When Françoise reached the age of nineteen, her parents decided it was time she should make her début in society. The parting must have been a severe trial for Madame de Fouquesolles, for her life had been to a large extent centred on this beautiful girl now ready to take her place in the world. Madame saw in her, with a certain pride as of her own handiwork, that perfect poise between the things of time and the things of eternity which marks the true Christian aristocrat. The youthful tendency to be critical and even caustic had been corrected, but the freshness of spontaneity had not been staled: grace and Christian courtesy—the breath of grace—were in every lineament of her character. Her social preparation, too, had been perfect, so that she knew the *Code de Présentation* in a society where the first and greatest social commandment was: Thou shalt please by bringing us your grace, your beauty, and—without which we will not receive you— your gaiety. Society still valued the poise and polish that had characterized the *grand siècle* of Louis XIV, when swords changed from weapons to ornaments, when women assumed a sort of omnipotence, when language became a search for the precision, the purity, the abstraction in which the classic spirit of Corneille, Molière, la Rochefoucauld and Madame de Sevigné was born. Talleyrand, who drank deep at the fountain of his times, said in a celebrated phrase: "Whoever has not lived before 1789 cannot know the sweetness of living." The whole emphasis of aristocratic France was on the art of living: the great talent of the century was *l'art du savoir-vivre*. The social rules were many and exacting, and required gifts from nature as well as self-polish. Into that world Françoise Blin de Bourdon glided gracefully, and gracefully took her place. When she came to write her memoirs, she is disappointingly silent on this period in her life. However, we are fortunate in having an eye-witness account of the impression made by Françoise on society. In the Archives of the Institute at Namur, the following is found among the *Souvenirs des Contemporaines*:

" Mademoiselle de Gézaincourt was quickly appreciated and eagerly sought in these reunions. Her lively and penetrating mind and her spirited conversation gave great pleasure. . . . The moral influence which she very soon acquired in that choice society gave her the right to speak in favour of religion, even before avowed partisans of Voltaire. Her observations were never taken amiss, for they were made in so gracious and delicate a manner that she won all hearts."

Françoise Blin de Bourdon was, therefore, a great success in society, good men sought her hand in marriage, and it is little wonder if she was swept a little more than she had intended along the enchanting flood of youth and wit and joy. But everything in her development had conspired to place a drop of divine discontent in the heart of the débutante, a divine canker in the flourishing rose of her world. Contemplation, the earth's most vital power, had touched her soul in the Benedictine prayer-laden atmosphere of Saint-Michel. It met her, in the pomp of her own milieu, at her moment of greatest social triumph, the moment of her presentation to Louis XVI and his Queen, Marie Antoinette. The star of the young couple was in its apogee, patriotic ovations constantly testified to their popularity—yet round the corner the guillotine awaited them, when the fleurs-de-lis would be trampled in blood by a drunken mob. But just now, the glory and brilliance of the court of Louis XVI was the envy of the crowned heads of Europe: and yet, in its heart, it

held a greater glory than any regal pomp, for by the
throne of Louis was his sister, the saintly Madame
Elizabeth of France, known to history as "the most
touching victim of the Revolution." The early companions of Françoise in religion have left it on record
that the only subject on which she would speak, concerning those years, was that of Madame Elizabeth.
There are psychic affinities between certain souls, and
soul speaks to soul without human language, just as a
harp string that is plucked is said to echo in other harp
strings, though a hand has not been laid upon them.
The gracious piety and the regal dignity of Madame
Elizabeth made a deep impression on Françoise, and
the Princess was very favourably impressed by her. Had
she so desired, Françoise could have taken her place in
the group that moved, socially and morally, with
Madame Elizabeth. But there was a certain vague
unrest in the heart of the girl that would not allow her
to do so, because her soul was too noble to be content
with the things that lay within her reach. There was
a conflict in her soul, not so much the conflict between
good and evil which she shared with all of us, but
between good and better, and even between better and
best: such a conflict as Oxenham had in mind when he
said: "To every man there openeth a way, and ways
—and a Way." She has little to say about this conflict,
but an entry in her notes is very significant. Under
the year 1783 she writes: "Imperfect light, half-
conversion."

The shadow of death was on the year 1784 for
Françoise. Late in the previous year, her mother fell
from her carriage and, after a long illness, died April
2nd, 1784, with a blessing in her soul for the daughter
who had nursed her with loving care. In February,
the news of the death of the Baron de Fouquesolles had
reached Bourdon. As a result, Françoise returned to
Gézaincourt to be the companion and consoler of her

grandmother. Long hours at her mother's sick-bed had begun to bring into prominence the deeper things in Françoise. The girl of nineteen who had left Gézaincourt with the courage and the long thoughts of youth, ripe to conquer her world, returned there quiet, chastened, clothed with an austere beauty. There was one great shadow on her peace. Her father, under the influence of Voltaire, had become a free-thinker. His salvation would come through a daughter who was to bury herself in a great silent manor-house for ten years to comfort a lonely woman; who would earn for herself from her heaped-up kindnesses to the peasants of her estate, the beautiful title "Angel of the château"; so that her prayers and her charity would finally prevail with God against all the sophisms of Ferney. Meantime, God was preparing Françoise for co-operation in a great work. That preparation was God's invariable one of silence and the cross, of Nazareth and Calvary. Gézaincourt was her Nazareth: the Revolution would be her Calvary.

Chaos, as we have seen, was unleashed in France in 1789. Four years later the name of the Citoyen Blin-Bourdon was listed among the *émigrés* in the department of Pas-de-Calais. Far from being an *émigré*, the Viscount Blin de Bourdon, an old man of eighty, loved and respected by his people, had not even left his village for two years. His son wrote a courageous letter pointing this out. As a result, the Viscount was thrown into prison at Amiens, and his son was served with a like sentence for supposed complicity with his aunt in smuggling funds to her *émigré* husband. And so the mad riot went on and on.

The Jacobin raid on Gézaincourt in which the Viscount was taken, made the Curé of the parish anxious for the safety of the Blessed Sacrament in the chapel of the château. He removed the Sacred Species, and placed them in a secret place in the house, and, since his life was one of danger and hiding, he appointed the two ladies as special custodians. This added touch of intimacy with her Eucharistic Lord was invaluable to Françoise. All her leisure was given to secret reparatory prayer before her Lord. Then her own hour came.

One night in February 1794, when the silence was about her and the deeper silence of Eucharistic adoration in her soul, there was a banging at the gate, the sound of iron on stone as horses were reined, and the air was suddenly hideous with thick and arrogant voices. Françoise was powerless for a second: then, recovering, she breathed a prayer of confidence in her hidden Lord, arose, went down to the gate and opened it. The lanterns which the "Agents of the Nation" held high, revealed, not a pale, frightened girl, but an aristocrat, erect and proud, who asked them in a level voice what this disturbance meant. There were centuries in that look and that voice, and before them they cringed. Then they stammered out something about an order to arrest the Baroness de Fouquesolles and herself. Meantime, like the leap of terror through a crowded street, the news that their "mothers" were in danger had spread panic through the village. Already the soldiers were surrounded by an angry peasantry, their weapons naked, ready to spring, at the slightest hint of danger to their loved ones. The confusion was growing and the mood of the villagers was getting more dangerous with every second's delay. A quick parley was held and a proposal made to Françoise. If the "Citoyenne Blin" would dismiss her people, and come away secretly with them, they would leave Madame de Fouquesolles in peace. Françoise agreed. She turned to her people with queenly dignity, thanked them, assured them that their benefactress would not be taken from them, and asked them to go quietly to their homes. With great reluctance they did so.

About midnight, when all was quiet, Françoise was placed in an open farm cart drawn by four farm horses. "The night was so dark," says the *Memoirs de Sr. Stephanie Warnier*, "that it was impossible to see anything except the menacing group surrounding the prisoner." When she asked where they were bringing her, she was told bluntly that she was under the protection of the Nation. The horror of her situation was suddenly with her, almost as though that horror sat hideously beside her, ringed by those hideous faces. "I felt all the shrinking and cowering of nature at the announcement of a certain and violent death," she said later. "But these moments of anguish soon passed; I made the sacrifice of my life to God, and begged for courage and resignation. This prayer brought calm to my soul." About eight o'clock in the morning, the *cortège* arrived at the gate of Amiens. Mademoiselle Françoise was escorted to a prison with the strange name, "La Providence." Here she learned that her father and several members of her family had been arrested. Her guards turned a deaf ear to her pleas to be allowed to join them.

From an English lady's journal—*Un Séjour en France*—of these years, we can reconstruct the scene of "La Providence" and savour its atmosphere, a strange blend of elegance and overcrowding. More than six hundred were heaped into a building intended to house less than half that number. The winter of 1794 was particularly severe, but no fires were allowed. Those to whom the use of mattresses was permitted had to spread them on the floor: sleeping arrangements were both primitive and spartan. Yet, in spite of these miseries, a certain contentment, a determination to make the best of things, prevailed among the prisoners. Musical instruments were played; they dressed with great care, and even exchanged visits according to the rules of society, as though the Revolution had never happened. A space was cleared, and three or four beds were piled together to make a gambling table for the bucks. "The bucks of the prison," writes the lady to whom we are indebted for our details, "who spent every morning penning piteous petitions for liberty, passed their evenings celebrating, in mock heroic verses, their fortune at cards." Between the musical instruments, the chatter of the women, the noise from the card tables, the declaiming of mock heroics, Françoise must have had a very trying time, since ten years of silence and recollection had given her a climate of soul to which all this was alien. The thoughtless frivolity around her hurt her deeply. "My greatest sorrow in those evil days," she said later, "was the great difficulty of preserving my soul quiet with God."

Meantime, at Gézaincourt, they were making every effort to keep the news of her grand-daughter's arrest from Madame de Fouquesolles. But it was impossible to continue inventing answers to her only and constant question, and at last they told her the sad truth. The blow was a terrible one. Her mind began to wander. She pushed all food from her, with the pathetic words: "I shall wait for my little one." But the little one never came, and Madame de Fouquesolles, worn out with age and grief, gradually sank and passed to her reward in heaven, there to await the grandchild whom she had expected so vainly on earth. The isolation and cry of loneliness in the old lady's death, rent the heart of Françoise. Even after many years had passed, she could not speak of that death except in a voice heavy with tears. "Ah, how God must reward her in the unshadowed happiness of heaven," she used to say. "She was so good, my poor grandmother."

The gendarmes were continuing to pile prisoners into already congested places, and soon something had to be done about "La Providence." The choice was given to the prisoners of remaining huddled together as they were, or of dividing so that some of them should live in the Carmel of Amiens. Contact with religion seems to have been thought even more uncomfortable than any overcrowding, for Françoise was the only volunteer. It was a happy change for her, since it was a change to her own atmosphere of recollection and prayer. Mère Marie de Saint Jean-Baptiste, a saintly and vigorous nun, had re-established formal religious life in her decimated community. Behind the usual brief comment in her notes, we can sense the strengthening and consolidating of a religious vocation in Françoise by contact with the purity of contemplative prayer. " My stay with the good Carmelites," she says, " did me much good."

In June 1794, André Dumont, fat, gross, but not bloody, was recalled from the directorship of Amiens to answer a charge of leniency and moderation. In his place came Joseph Lebon angry, as a mad bull that has tasted blood, with everything that had nobility or virtue in it. He dined grossly with the hangmen, and on his table stood a miniature guillotine made with flowers. His animal mind thought this the very cream of jest. His orgies were interrupted for the splendid spectacle of La Belle Guillotine having her daily meal, or to tick off the names of to-morrow's victims as though the list were her menu card. Every day a list of victims was read aloud in the prisons. Cries and lamentations followed: or wild rejoicing that life was to go on for another day. Heading one of these lists was the name —Françoise Blin de Bourdon, with the names of her father and her brother beside it. Her reaction is recorded in her notes. She writes:

" Accustomed though I was to look death in the face, this certainty of my impending execution, together with the thought of my father and brother, whom I should see only on the scaffold, caused me for a time an agony of pain. The bitterness of death passed over me, but it was soon at an end. The mercy of my God delivered my soul from this anguish, and with the aid of His supporting grace I regained, after a few moments, my usual serenity—only my prayers were longer and more earnest for help in the last awful moment."

But the supreme moment had not yet come. There was a delay in the executions, and in that delay Robespierre fell. The Reign of Terror was over. Among the first prisoners to be released were those in Les Carmélites. The nephew of Mademoiselle de Gézaincourt ran joyfully to the convent to announce that his aunt was free. "My child," she answered calmly, "I have made my evening prayer. To-morrow I shall join my father and you." Is it possible to hear in those words, at the moment of liberation, an undertone of regret? Perhaps she was thinking of her own case, too, when she wrote later of Julie Billiart: "She regretted having missed the opportunity of giving her life in testimony to her faith, with the result that she can be called a martyr by desire and will." . . . The union next day between father, son and daughter was one of intense joy. Afterwards, the Viscount Blin set out for his château at Bourdon. Françoise decided to stay for a year in the family mansion of her brother, the Hôtel de la rue des Augustins—a name which every follower of Julie Billiart must hear with reverence. For in this decision of Françoise, God wrote finis to the first part of a glorious design, since by it, the seemingly chance meeting was to take place between Françoise and Julie Billiart.

Two souls had been led, each through its own Nazareth and its own Calvary, to give full significance to this meeting. In each case, God had again "written straight with crooked lines," because His ways are not our ways. He would use a hunted, helpless invalid,

E

stripped of all but God, and an aristocrat of nature and of grace, to perform a great work.

Already the soil of that work was seeded with the martyr's blood, which, both from Julie Billiart and Françoise Blin de Bourdon, God had accepted in the vehemence of their desires.

CHAPTER FIVE

THE DESIGN TAKES SHAPE

SHORTLY after Françoise had taken up residence in the rue des Augustins, a woman for whom life had become a shrivelled husk, knocked at the door seeking a place where she could bury herself with her sorrow. She had watched the sun glinting on the guillotine blade as it descended on the prostrate body of her father: and immediately after she watched her husband take his place. She turned away with a broken heart and in utter desolation of soul. She wandered distractedly for a while, and finally made her tear-filled way to a place where friendship might soothe and console her. The door of the Hôtel Blin opened wide in welcome to the distracted Madame Baudoin, whom, "with her three bright girls," we have met before at the bedside of Julie Billiart in Cuvilly. Once established with Françoise, her thoughts turned more and more to the saintly invalid. She had a great longing to see her. There was a little unused set of apartments in the house that would suit Julie and Felicity very well, and Madame Baudoin pleaded with Julie until she had obtained her promise to come. In Françoise's account of her arrival, we get a pathetic impression of how frail and emaciated twenty-two years of bedridden suffering had left Julie. "Arrived at Amiens," she writes, "her niece took her in her arms and carried her to the bed that had been prepared." Felicity had not a heavy burden to carry.

Some days later, Madame Baudoin, already consoled, calm, more resigned, brought Françoise Blin de

Bourdon to visit the saintly invalid. It is natural that the biographer should wish to linger over a moment so fraught with the future. Perhaps the most wonderful facet of this meeting between the co-Foundresses of the Institute of Notre Dame, is that Julie did not cry out with joy when she looked up at that face bent compassionately towards her. For as she looked, her vision must have been again before her, so that, in that first moment of meeting, Françoise stood by her bedside in the habit of Notre Dame, with the shadow of the cross upon her. How otherwise explain the firm confidence with which she later assured Françoise that the Institute was God's will for her because she had seen her clearly "among ours at Compiègne." But Julie kept all her joy in her heart, knowing that God has His own plans and His own times. A great joy of confirmation was in Julie's heart, because the other faces about her were not the faces of her vision. The most glowing part of her vision had become real.

Françoise's feelings at this first meeting were mixed. She felt drawn to the invalid by something peaceful and holy in her every feature: yet, as she confessed later, she felt a certain repugnance due especially to the difficulty of holding a conversation with her and to the unlovely sounds which her poor, contracted jaws caused her to make when trying to speak. She came back again and again, that she might sit and read to Julie, and that she might feel the love of God growing in her heart through contact with such glowing purity. Thus was born a friendship that can serve as a model for all religious friendship, since it was founded and centred in a mutual glowing love of God. The essence of their friendship is expressed in a splendid paragraph from a letter of Julie's to Françoise a year later:

" Never, my dear good friend, could I tell you half the good wishes with which my heart is overflowing for you. It is in

"BEHOLD THE SPIRITUAL DAUGHTERS WHOM I GIVE YOU
IN THE INSTITUTE WHICH I PROMISE TO MARK WITH MY
CROSS"

the Heart of our good Jesus in the Crib that we must meet, you and I, and there learn all the hard lessons of humility, death to self, complete renunciation. It is there in His Heart that I give you rendezvous, that I want constantly to meet you."

Her New Year greeting, in the same letter, is typical of such a friendship:

"May the New Year be fraught for you with graces and blessings and marked spiritual progress. This is what I very specially wish for you . . . that God may grant you the grace to appreciate fully the doctrine of the Cross so that you may arrive at the goal of all your desires. Entire death to self is the grace that I ask for you, and I trust that you will beg the same grace for me."

There is a spiritual freshness in such a friendship which neither age nor the grave itself can make stale. Françoise was obliged to reside, from 1795 to 1797, sometimes at Gézaincourt, sometimes at Bourdon, and this caused an exchange of letters between the two friends from which we can reconstruct a fairly accurate picture of life in the rue des Augustins in these years.

It is immediately evident from these letters that the household had its spiritual centre in Julie. Indeed, she was soon surrounded by a group of young ladies of very good will, who might seem to be material for her great work: but Julie knew that there was no substance in that group, that it was but as the foam-pattern that forms for a time on the swirl of the waters, only to break up again and dissolve. They were not the faces of the vision.

Apart from Felicity, the member of the group whose general characteristics are most in evidence is Lise, the youngest daughter of the Countess Baudoin. Vivacious and beautiful, she would come into the sick-room with a lightness and gaiety that was like a ray of sunshine to Julie. They became very attached to each other, but Julie, with that gift of spiritual analysis which characterized her, saw a certain volatility, a tendency to undisciplined extremes, which gave her cause to fear, "I am very pleased with my little Lise; she is a little angel at present. She clings to the good God as much as possible." . . . But very soon there is a note of anxiety in another letter to Françoise: "You know, my dear good friend, I am always desirous to do what the good God wants, but I must confide to you at this moment that Mlle Lise is doing very well and I should be very distressed if the change (to Paris) was harmful to her. If you could persuade Monsieur and Madame Blin to leave their suite of rooms to the Baudoins at Easter, I could remain at Amiens with Lise." Her fears for this beautiful and unbalanced seventeen-year-old girl were well-founded. When Françoise—or Mère Blin, as she was then—came to sum up her impression of Lise, she remembered her as gracious, very temperamental, drawn violently both ways by a love of pleasure and dissipation, and by a genuine attraction towards God. Pleasure seems to have won the day, and there is a hint of some frustration in the last reference of Mère Blin to Lise—a sentence that seems a sigh and the drawing of a curtain of charitable silence. "Lise, too, married," she writes, "but I fear not according to her vocation." We turn from Lise with a sense of the pity of it all: for she seemed a lovely and a lovable child.

Lise had four friends a little older than herself: Josephine and Gabrielle Doria, Jeanne and Aglae du Fos de Méry, whom she brought to visit Julie. They immediately fell under her influence, and, after the death of Madame Baudoin, came to live in the same house with her. From that time, they lived as a little religious community, giving much edification to those about them. "They observed a little rule exactly," writes Mère Blin in her Memoirs, "recited together the Office of the Blessed Virgin, had all things in common, and called Julie ' Ma Mère.' Indeed," she goes on, "it seemed a beginning to the work Julie was to accomplish; but these first plants sent down no roots, some because a taste for worldly things was but lulled in their hearts, others because inordinate love of relations drew them away. And thus the little group was dispersed." One of the Doria sisters became a nun in the Visitation Order at Paris. Her sister married, as Mère Blin said, "according to her vocation." In recounting the fate of Aglae de Méry, Mère Blin's quiet narrative seems suddenly to stiffen with horror. "The younger of the Méry sisters," she writes, "who like Lise, was also called by God, after having passed a couple of years with a sister whom she loved inordinately and who had poured out her soul on all that was worldly, fell from her early fervour, and died a horrible death, without the Sacraments, crying out that abominations were crowding about her bed." It is the old, sad story that the refusal to answer a call to scale the heights may mean that a soul flings itself into the depths, the horror in the words *Corruptio optimi pessima*. It lies as a saddening shadow and a salutary warning in the vestibule of Notre Dame.

What of Felicity, the faithful niece and nurse, in these years? Her name figures frequently in the letters, particularly when the writer is giving some intimate details to her absent friend. A conversationally intimate letter of October 21st, 1795, gives us a delightful feeling of being one of the group by the bedside.

"Now I must tell you something about my household affairs or you will not be satisfied. My little Felicity works as hard as she can, day and night, in order to provide us with bread. This is getting dearer every day. . . . Nor can she always get the material she needs. They wish to sell her cloth at 20 sous a yard; she had bought ten yards. This will last her for some weeks; then she wants to go to Compiègne to see what she can buy there. If she goes, I shall be all alone again, and yet, unless she works, she cannot support me. . . .

"You know that Madame (Baudoin) is in Paris. I have not heard a word from her since she left. She has not left me so much as a single penny. You see how good God is to have given to my little Felicity a talent for sewing. We two are never weary of thanking God for this."

This quotation, more than any comment, serves to underline the utter helplessness of Julie, and her child-like dependence on Felicity for all her wants. The next letter in which we get a revelation of these years, is that of December 23rd. Madame Baudoin has seemingly returned from Paris, but in her absence a stove had been put in their apartments, and this, we gather, was all to the good: Felicity, we are told, "is now quite at peace," from which we may gather that the perennial problem of two women and one kitchen was not unknown in the rue des Augustins *ménage*. Julie writes:

"Winter is a very trying time for me, as you know. I have these fainting spells of which I have spoken to you. I am cured of the tertian ague but not of the nervous fever. Would you believe that the cessation of the ague has left me with a continual need for food? The good God, as a good Father, provides for everything. We can manage our own house-keeping entirely now. Since we have had a stove, Felicity does not to go Madame's kitchen at all, and, as a result, is now quite at peace."

This stove figures again in a letter dated "Last day of the year 1795," and it is even held to be an added inducement to her friend to come to her:

"A little word about our household affairs. . . . You will find everything needful in the holy poverty of our house. You will live there as you wish. We have a stove for our cooking —indeed, one can make excellent soup on it—and we have wood to keep the oven going. Felicity has eggs and she will make you whatever you like, with great pleasure. . . ."

A new and very valuable addition was made to the household in the rue des Augustins. Madame Baudoin had known a good priest in Paris called Monsieur Thomas, and now, hunted by the hate of the Revolutionaries, he had taken refuge in Amiens where the persecution was a little less severe. Nevertheless, he had still to take many precautions by hiding his name, his priesthood, and often himself, from the watchful and avaricious eyes that were everywhere. Madame. brought him to Julie, and very soon he became her spiritual guide, philosopher and friend. Life brightened for Julie with the brightness it had when the dew was on the grass and the glory in the flower: Monsieur Thomas carried her Eucharistic Lord to her every day, and the joy she had not known since those early days in Cuvilly—her intense joy in daily Communion—was hers again. When the Bretagne ladies with whom Monsieur lodged left Amiens, he came to live with Monsieur Blin, in a little room close to that of Julie. No time was lost in erecting a temporary altar in the saintly invalid's room, where Monsieur Thomas said Holy Mass every day. Her joy was complete. Danger was around them on all sides, and hence the altar and every evidence of the Holy Sacrifice had to be carefully removed immediately after the celebration. This danger and the constant vexations it occasioned, caused Monsieur Thomas, Mère Julie and Mademoiselle Blin to leave for Bettencourt, a country place about six leagues from Amiens, where Mademoiselle Doria had offered them a little château. They left quietly in darkness on June 16th, 1799. . . . The first grouping in the rue des Augustins was now at an end: but its very dissolution served only to underline the reason of its being. All this had happened that a powerful spiritual friendship might be born, and in the warmth of that friendship, God was soon to build.

"The country air," writes Mère Blin, "did not restore Julie to health or give her back the use of her legs, rather it caused her a severe spell of sickness. However, she gathered sufficient strength to be able to sit in a kind of invalid chair, so that she no longer remained habitually in bed. Moreover, she began to recover a more frequent and clearer use of her speech. Every morning, Monsieur Thomas asked her several questions and commanded her to speak her answers. Obedience caused her to make great efforts which, little by little, restored the habit of speech, and, though she would often be silent, she did not relapse into dumbness before night, as formerly. Towards the end of her time in Bettencourt, Monsieur Thomas made a journey to his native Normandy, and during his absence, the good God restored to our Mother the complete and free use of speech which she needed, now more than ever, in order that she might instruct."

Such a need to instruct, as the same chronicler remarks elsewhere, was as the need for food: she could scarcely have lived without it. A clear, unbroken line of instruction and guidance of souls runs through her tortured years, right back to the days when she told her parable to the children, and Monsieur l'Abbé Dangicourt stood in the shadows, listening, with a Magnificat in his soul. Julie Billiart had always been a teacher. Now God had restored to her the gift of speech that she might use it for His glory. Moreover, He was about to send her a priest who would see in Julie the power and the instrument he was seeking for the re-birth of religion in France. He would turn to Julie, and in the name of God, would give her a clear command.

The affairs of his Congregation had brought Père Varin, Superior of the Fathers of the Faith, to Bettencourt, and he was immediately overpowered with joy at the sight of the work of instruction launched by Julie and Françoise among the inhabitants of the little town. Père Varin was fired with one great ideal. A heavy fog of ignorance was the legacy of the Revolution to France, and the mass of the people were irreligious, but only because they were groping. The remedy to hand was scarcely adequate, for the Revolution had sadly thinned the ranks of those who devoted their lives to Christian education. Père Varin was no defeatist: everywhere he went, he preached and inculcated by every means the need for a tremendous revival of religious education in France. Julie Billiart must have come into his life like an inspiration and an answer to prayer. In the Chronicle of the early years, Mère Blin records:

"Sometimes ecclesiastics would come from Amiens to see Monsieur Thomas, and one of these is of great importance to us because he was the cause of the birth of our Institute, and its early prop. When he had gained a deep insight into our Mère Julie, he judged, against overwhelming evidence to the contrary, that she was destined to work for the glory of God in a far more extensive field, and he spoke to her as to one so called. But how can such things be, she exclaimed. . . . And, in truth, they seemed very remote. The first instrument of Providence for our foundation was Monsieur Joseph (Varin), a zealous priest filled with the spirit of God."

The rest of this quotation shows how effective the words and enthusiasm of Père Varin had been:

"For when the last of the Revolution had passed, at the end of February 1803, we returned to Amiens. The accommodation in the house of Monsieur Blin was not available, and the only residence we could find was a small house in the rue du Puits Abrandi, which had no garden, was inconvenient in every way, and was the cause of much suffering to our Mother. As usual, however, she held catechism lessons and gathered the children about her. It was in this house that her niece left her, to marry a neighbouring school teacher. Monsieur Thomas brought his cousin, Constance Blondel, from Normandy, to replace Felicity in housekeeping. We were not six months in the little house. The divine goodness did not delay in giving us a bigger and more convenient house in the rue Neuve, and it is that house which we must regard as the cradle of the Institute."

The way to the rue Neuve had been for Julie Billiart

a long way, long with pain, sorrow, disappoinment. It seemed a lifetime since she had rushed home to her mother with the news that Monsieur l'Abbé wished her to receive her Eucharistic Lord. It seemed a far call from the almost helpless invalid to that swift and glowing child. Yet the design was complete, and, as we linger at the moment of its completion, it is right that our minds should turn again to Madame Billiart, now some years gone to her reward. She passes from these pages, but her influence, the untold influence of a good mother, lies in all that is to follow.

CHAPTER SIX

THE DESIGN TAKES FLESH

IN the Bettencourt years, the churches had been opened and public worship restored in France. To celebrate this, Pope Pius VII published a jubilee, and the Fathers of the Faith, with Père Varin at their head, began the Great Missions which were to be the first big external impetus given to the teaching vocation of Julie Billiart and the Institute of Notre Dame. Père Varin had seen the tremendous power latent in the zeal of these two good ladies, Julie and Françoise, and he now urged them to set about recruiting others under the fine banner they had tentatively unfurled under a sky grown grey with ignorance. He told them, in words which were warm with conviction, that those desires to lead and to teach had a breadth of meaning greater than they knew: that they would indeed saturate and seed the dry and stony places of France. It seemed incredible to these two simple souls that, through them, a wilderness was to blossom: yet, in the simplicity that was to remain always the secret of their strength, they began a Novena to Our Lady to obtain postulants. They had moved to the house in the rue Neuve on the feast of Our Lady of the Snow, 1803. They now knelt at her feet with the whiteness of their virgin desires about them, that she might do with them and with their desires whatever was to the greater glory of her Son. The simplicity of the *Ecce Ancilla Domini* was in their souls. Mary saw it as something of her own, and raised her hand in immaculate blessing over it. In that blessing, Notre Dame was born. Mary

obtained an answer from her Son. Postulants presented
themselves, but they were not from the ranks of the
rich and mighty. Mary, as it were, gathered them from
the street in Nazareth.

The first to come was Catherine Duchâtel of Rheims.
"She left the Maison de l'Oratoire," says the early
Chronicle, "where some girls were being prepared to
undertake the education of young ladies. Catherine
Duchâtel felt a greater leaning towards the poor than
towards these young ladies, and accordingly she left
the Ladies of the Sacred Heart and came to us. She
remained with us but one year; her health, which was
bad when she came, and which quickly became worse,
caused her to return to the Oratoire, where she died
six months later." In Candlemas of that year, 1804,
however, Catherine had joined with Julie Billiart and
Françoise Blin in kneeling before the Blessed Sacrament, with Père Varin as witness, and making a vow
of chastity and a vow to devote themselves to the Christian education of girls. Less than eighteen months
later, Catherine was dead: yet her moments of contact
with the beginnings of Notre Dame had the timeless
significance of a deeply spiritual soul. "I believe,"
writes Mère Blin, "that we can regard her as our protectress before God." Other souls, too, came to the
banner unfurled in Mary's name: Justine Garçon and
Victoire Leleu, both highly gifted and extremely
spiritual souls. Victoire Leleu is specially mentioned
in the annals as she was destined to be one of the pillars
of the Institute. "By what name shall I call her?"
writes Mère Blin when, twenty years later, she came
to announce her death to the Sisters. "I shall call her
Charity, Purity, Simplicity, Gentleness, Courtesy."
Such, indeed, was Victoire, and it is in the strength of
these virtues, in her soul and in the souls of the others,
that the mighty design of Notre Dame was made flesh.

The Feast of the Purification should have a special

domestic significance for the Sisters of Notre Dame. On the Feast of the Purification, 1804, the first members took their vows, and received from Père Varin the first draft of a provisional rule. The following year, on the same feast, they received a fuller, more detailed version of the same provisional rule, and again "we vowed ourselves to the Heart of Jesus, under the protection of the Heart of Mary, that same day."

"It was Candlemas, 1806," writes one of her biographers, "and the community was, according to custom, gathered round Mère Julie in the work-room for the evening 'Instruction' in Christian doctrine. Julie spoke in burning words of the mystery of the day, and then all at once intoned with extraordinary joy of spirit the canticle of Simeon, which was taken up by her daughters. *Lumen ad revelationen gentium*, sang the Sisters, when suddenly Julie's voice broke, her eyes fixed themselves on the crucifix in a rapt gaze of love, her countenance glowed with light. The whole community saw her thus in ecstasy, raised above the ground, motionless, inundated with the very beatitude of heaven. It is a constant tradition in the Institute that in this rapture God had shown His servants that her children should one day cross the seas and oceans, to carry the light of revelation to nations sitting in darkness and in the shadow of death. The vision has seen its fulfilment."

There is a profound significance in this vision of their holy Mother transfigured, accorded to her first little group of followers. In a few calm days before the awful storm of His Passion broke about Him and His followers, Christ showed Himself in His glory to His chosen Apostles on Thabor, that they might be strengthened for the doubts and disillusionments ahead, dry as the dust on the road to Emmaus. As so often in the lives of the saints, there was a Gospel-echo here in the life of Julie Billiart. Her vision had assured her that the Institute she would found was to be marked with a cross. A few halcyon days were given to her in which to establish her work, and then the chalice of bitterness would again be raised to her lips, brimmed with the gall and wormwood of the worst of all persecution—persecution by the just. In those days of calm, it was fitting that her followers should be strengthened by the glimpse of a glory of soul no misrepresentation or slander could tarnish, in order that they might believe in her, in her darkest hour.

The priest whom we first met as the friend of Madame Baudoin, Monsieur Thomas, was still with them, still voicing a clear certainty that Julie Billiart was to be one of the greatest means of promoting God's glory, and absolutely unshaken in this certainty by her continued powerlessness and infirmity. With Père Lambert and Père Enfantin, who were lodged in the rue Neuve, he was among those who were conducting the Mission. The Sisters attended the Mission, Mère Julie being carried in a sedan chair, and moreover they were very valuable co-operators in the labour for souls. The Fathers entrusted them with the entire instruction and preparation for the sacraments of the women and girls who thronged the Mission, and thus the first great shaping was given to the work of Notre Dame.

Père Enfantin must now come into the foreground of our picture as the great instrument of heaven's favour to Julie. There had been nothing soft or easy about the priesthood of Père Enfantin. He had been ordained furtively at night, when the Reign of Terror was at its highest pitch of ferocity, and continued hardship had made his character one of granite, while his Savonarola-like, fiery eloquence swept through a people whom he had watched sinking into a quagmire of turpitude and indifference. The tenderness of his piety was as remarkable as the austerity of his life: but in his relations with Julie Billiart the austerity is very much in evidence. The times, Père Enfantin seems to have reasoned, needed men of iron, and therefore a will of iron must be put into this woman in whom he recognized one of the focal points for the re-birth of France. Not many years hence, Renan was to express the despair that was the legacy of the Revolution: "Young man, France is dying: trouble not her agony." That France was not dying, and has not died, is due under God to the unflinching courage of priests like Père Enfantin who stood amid the moral débris of a world flung down in man-made chaos, and said: France is dying through her own blind wilfulness: she must and can only be re-born through penance and pain. When Père Enfantin met a soul like that of Julie Billiart, he strove to plunge it into a crucible of pain that it might emerge utterly selfless, and therefore mighty to re-make a world nearer to the Heart of God. Humility must be the fibre of such a soul, and there is no surer way to humility than the way of humiliations. Therefore Père Enfantin heaped humiliations on Julie Billiart, and there seems little doubt that he sometimes exceeded the bounds of good sense in doing so (as when he ordered her to kill with her own hands a cat that had been her faithful companion for nearly fifteen years). During several years, he heaped scornful reproaches on her, but in this, as in other trials to which he was yet to subject her, we must see him as a stern prophet of God shaping a soul for a stern time.

One day, as Julie was making her laborious way, moving first one leg of her chair and then the other, Père Enfantin came to her and said in his usual brusque way: "I begin a Novena to-day to the Sacred Heart for a person in whom I am interested. You will join me in making it." Julie quietly assented, and continued on her way. When she reached the stairs, she began the ritual of pain to which her infirmity condemned her. Slowly she edged herself till she sat on the stair nearest her, and then she pushed herself painfully up by sitting on each stair. At the top a chair was kept always in readiness, and by means of it she made her way to the

F

chapel, where she began her Novena for the unknown intention. The fifth day of the Novena was the first of June, and the first Friday of the month. Mère Julie was in the garden, alone, seated in her invalid chair. The door of the garden opened, and Père Enfantin came towards her with those long, purposeful strides so characteristic of him. He stood before her, and without any preliminary greeting he said in a firm, commanding voice: "If you have faith, rise and take a step in honour of the Heart of Jesus." Julie rose, and strength seemed suddenly to leap through her weak and crippled body. Steadily she took a step. "Take another," came the command. With joy beginning to sing its canticle within her, she took another step. "Yet a third," came the command. She did so. "That will do; sit down," came the final command, at the moment when Julie was overwhelmed with the realization that she could really walk. He commanded her to keep her cure a secret from all except Monsieur Thomas. "Shortly after this," says Mère Blin in her annals, "still seated on her chair and moving in her customary manner, she went to her ground-floor bed. The following morning she mounted the stairs in her usual way . . . but at the moment of Holy Communion, instead of dragging herself on her knees to the holy table, she rose and walked." We may add as a footnote to Mère Blin's account that the distance between her place and the Communion rail was small, and the recollection of the Sisters so perfect that the marvel passed unnoticed. "After Mass," the account goes on, "when we had all left the chapel, she went into the sacristy to Monsieur Thomas. She walked before him, and unable to contain his joy, he wept with all his heart. She continued to play the invalid for two days more, and walked only when she was certain of not being observed. On the Sunday of the Octave of Corpus Christi, she came in her chair with us to the street door at the moment when

LOOK! OUR MOTHER COMES AND SHE IS WALKING

the Procession of the Blessed Sacrament passed by, and she could have joined it but for the command to keep her cure secret."

We can sense a certain tension, as of the pull between hope and a settled resignation, in the community, during the four days that elapsed before the joyful news was announced to the Sisters. Some had noticed her walking the few steps to Communion on one or other of these days, but they wondered if it meant a complete cure, and they thought it might be a special favour given her at the moment of Communion, just as, some years since, a gift of speech had been given to her at the moment of Confession. Whatever their thoughts they respected her silence. So perfect was that silence and the obedience it signified, that Monsieur Thomas began to become incredulous. " But Mère Julie," the annals report him as saying, " I do not see you continue to walk. The works of God are perfect, so that if He cured you, you could still walk." "But," she replied, " I assure you that I feel in myself even while you speak to me, something which tells me that I can. Do you wish me to walk up the stairs before you? " "Yes," he replied. She did so with ease.

By the following Tuesday the ban on revealing her cure, which had undoubtedly been placed by Père Enfantin in pursuance of a plan to mortify Julie in every way, was lifted. The community had assembled for breakfast, grace had been said, and the meal begun. Two children were standing near the door. Suddenly their shrill, treble voices shattered the silence and recollection of the room: " Look! Our Mother comes and she is walking." . . . " We did not budge from our seats to greet her," records Mère Blin; " I know not by what dumb stupor we were seized. . . . Our good Mother came in with a firm step, and suddenly we cast ourselves on our knees, we retired immediately to the chapel, we chanted a *Te Deum* in fervent thanksgiving.

We did not enjoy her presence for long after her cure, because she went, almost immediately, into retreat. This lasted ten days, and was both a thanksgiving and preparation for her future work." Those short sentences, tumbling over each other in the Chronicle, give the impression of the Sisters doing now one thing, now another, not knowing how best to express their joy. And in the midst of that joy, Julie Billiart prayed that her infirmity might be given back to her if she was not to use her new-found health for the glory of God.

The name—"the saint"—which the child, Julie Billiart, had acquired in Cuvilly, remained with her at all times, because the impression made on all who came within her world was ever the same. "To have Mère Julie under the roof was a festival," testifies Madame Eugenie Ancelle, examined as a witness in the Process of Beatification; "so deep was the respect which she inspired that one felt inclined to kneel down before her." This general veneration and the great gifts of grace given her, put Père Enfantin on his guard against human complacency in his disciple. He began to assume an overbearing and, indeed, a bullying attitude towards her. Though cured, her stomach remained weak, and unable to retain certain types of food. He ordered her to make her meals of such food. To drink cold water caused her great stomach pains. Her director commanded her to drink a specially iced water into which he would sometimes mix ashes. He loaded her with reproaches, framed in words of sarcastic contempt: he would enter the community refectory and order her to kneel on the floor, and on one occasion went so far as to dash a glass of cold water full in her face. During her ten-day retreat he confined her to a garret, and almost shattered her newly acquired strength by penances heaped upon her. (These exaggerated manifestations of his zeal culminated in the stupid gaucherie of the cat incident, which, for crudity,

equals anything in the annals of the saints.) Indeed,
much could be said on the severity of his whole
approach to Julie Billiart, but it is more profitable to
view it as she herself did, that we may wonder at the
unbroken gleam of purest silver, which is the light of
her faith, of her obedience, of her magnificent simplicity, in all this murk. "The good God," she writes
later in a letter to her Sisters, "likes me to grope my
way along." To grope: she had indeed to grope: to
grope through years of dumbness and paralysis, to
grope through the soul's waste land of aridity, to grope
through human stupidity and exaggerated zeal, that she
might learn to grope her way through a dark tunnel of
calumny, of misrepresentation, of twisted words, of
actions stupidly misread, that she might finally emerge
into the light, and knock at the bridegroom's door, with
the white robe of her simplicity absolutely unsullied
by the mud-slinging through which her years had
wound. With such a background in mind, the apparently simple words in one of her letters take on a new
and living significance, since they make, as it were, a
palimpsest, with the meaning traced in deeds beneath
the words:

"Since the spirit of God is the spirit of simplicity, the surest
way for us is to keep ourselves in the attitude of mind which
approximates to the simplicity of faith, avoiding above all
things, all reasonings which lead to anxiety of mind, and
would cause us to lose peace of soul, our one great treasure."

After her retreat, the Fathers pressed Julie to accompany them to St.-Valéry-sur-Somme and to Abbeville.
Leaving the little community in the care of the co-
Foundress, she set off with Sister Anastasie (Leleu) to
continue in these places the good work she had done
in Amiens. Her letters are full of a simple, holy joy
in her work. . . . "I must finish my letter," she
writes on one occasion, "to go to a good man to whom I

am teaching the Credo. He is nearly seventy, and has not yet made his first Communion. He has the best will in the world." . . . "May the name of the Lord be praised and blessed in everything! What is certain, my dear daughters, is that the good God is always very good." Perhaps this particular eulogy of the goodness of God—though such eulogy fills both her letters and her conversation—was occasioned by an occurrence which was first a cross and then a glory. One day, as she was walking in the street at St.-Valéry, some horses frightened her and, in moving quickly aside, she sprained her foot severely. It blackened and was so painful that the Missioners, now very doubtful of her cure, thought of sending her back to Amiens. Anxious not to interrupt her work, Mère Julie dragged herself to the church, and spent several hours in prayer on her knees before the Blessed Sacrament. She walked from the church perfectly cured.

In September 1805, Père Thomas left Amiens for the Missions of the west and the south. He was soon followed by his energetic co-worker, Père Enfantin. The Missions were not popular in high quarters, for the imperial power, feeling its ground insecure, was quick to take umbrage at the religious demonstrations which accompanied the Missions. The Fathers of the Faith were looked on as an army of conspirators, and their Missions as merely a huge net-work of deep and treacherous plots against the new Emperor of the French. The Society of Père Varin was dispersed and their Missions suppressed. The Sisters must have felt the loss of Père Thomas, their father and friend for ten years, very keenly. Moreover, the interruption of the Missions had given to the Sisters the valuable boon of having both Père Thomas and Père Varin as their instructors. "The class-equipment was primitive in the extreme, and professors and pupils often lacked the most indispensable apparatus. Many a time did

THE SISTERS OF NOTRE DAME HAVE JUST OPENED FREE
SCHOOLS FOR LITTLE GIRLS

Père Varin and Père Thomas chalk out the sums and the geometrical problems on the floor." Vignettes like these, of the early days, are well worth preserving, so that at any time in its far-flung development, the followers of Julie Billiart may look back to the cradle of their Institute, and say: this, and the spirit animating it, *is* Notre Dame.

The little community grew in numbers, until, by 1806, the number in the community reached eighteen, and it became necessary to remove to a larger house in the Faubourg-Noyon. The number of children, however, had dwindled to four, as situations had been found for those who had been trained. Then Mère Julie adopted an expedient, both effective and picturesque. She sent a novice and a postulant in different directions among the poor streets that huddled about the Faubourg-Noyon, with instructions to keep ringing a bell and to cry out: "The Sisters of Notre Dame have just opened free schools for little girls. Go and tell your parents the news." Grubby little faces were lifted in wonder, and little feet scurried about with the news. On the first day sixty children presented themselves, and the numbers went on increasing daily. They were met with a warmth of charity which must at first have amazed these little rough and tumbles, and then bound them in deep affection to their teachers. They were lucky children, favoured to be a new warmth in the Church of Christ. The timid echoes of that little bell in the doors and alley-ways round the Faubourg-Noyon, made but faint ripples in the world's great sea of sound: but they had in them that strange power of simplicity and humbleness of heart, which would make them heard in many, far-flung lands, in the great pulse of a new, spiritual re-birth.

Notre Dame was now like a bud, big with the exuberance of spring, its core a first fine rapture of fervour and self-abnegation. The community of the

Faubourg-Noyon lived a life of spartan simplicity. "The food was that of the very poor: for breakfast, dry bread and water; for dinner, soup and a dish of vegetables, except on Sundays when there was a little meat. Even so, it was necessary to keep an eye on the more fervent, lest they should retrench on what was barely sufficient. The dormitory was constructed by running up partitions in the attic; palliasses laid on the floors were the beds." The beginnings of a religious movement destined to bear lasting fruit must be of a great spiritual strength. In details like these, we get the evidence of that strength, and we sense the deep interior spirit of prayer that gave courage to mould all these hard things into beauty.

"What is the Institute of Notre Dame?" Cardinal Sterckx, Archbishop of Mechlin, asks. "I answer: It is a breath of the Apostolic Spirit fallen from the Heart of Jesus upon the heart of a woman who believed and who loved." The emphasis on the interior life is constant in the letters of Julie Billiart, because she knew that all apostolic energy is but useless beating of the air, unless it is an overflow from the prayerful contemplation of Divine Truth. Without it, she writes in one of her letters, we build our spiritual house of dust, and the dust is "borne away with the wind." Nothing is left but the arid disillusionment of those who try to fashion the things of God with hands of clay that have not first been dipped deep till they are made new with prayer. In a remarkable phrase, she writes: "If I have not souls which *grapple themselves to the good God* with their whole heart, our society will crumble away." She urges them to seed their hours with ejaculatory prayer: "I would counsel you to fill your day with ejaculatory prayer; that is a practice which helps the interior life." Again: "If you do not become *souls of prayer*, our Institute will perish"; and her famous maxim—"*Courtes confessions, longues*

oraisons" ("Short confessions, long prayers")—is this
emphasis on the necessity of prayer, in four words of
great, good common sense. This interior life was to
breed a very positive outlook, and in one of her letters
she insists that the cultivation of one's own spiritual
garden is at best but half the task: "One who enters
our society must have far other intentions than merely
to escape the dangers of the world. Our chief aim is
the glory of God and the salvation of souls. . . . My
dear Sisters, you are not made for yourselves alone; the
principal end of our Institute is to propagate God's
glory. Ah! how happy are you, dear Sisters, to be
called to the office of the Apostles, nay, of Christ Himself." In another letter, she echoes the sentiment of
St. Francis de Sales, that one soul is diocese enough for
a Bishop: "Who knows but that God gathered us all
together here to win Him one single soul? And would
it not be a great thing to put one soul on the way of
salvation—a soul which cost the Blood of God! "

The autumn of the year 1806 saw the religious family
of Julie Billiart grown to thirty in number. In the
following year, an imperial decree granted a provisional
approbation to the new Institute. The time had come
to move to other fields, where a harvest, white for reap-
ing, beckoned to this zealous group of God's chosen
ones. Père Leblanc, to whom Père Varin had entrusted
the care of the Sisters of Notre Dame, had occasion to
make an official visit to one of his colleges between
Bruges and Courtrai, and he invited Julie to accompany him. No sooner had she set foot on Belgian soil
than the Bishop of Ghent at once asked her to make
a foundation in his diocese. One of the most remarkable natural gifts of Julie Billiart was a great cautious
common sense, a gift that is country-bred, born of the
patience of the life of the soil, where the seed is sown,
the shoot comes, then the blade, then the harvest, with
nature's unhurried rhythm. This cautious common

sense is seen in her answer to the Bishop, for her agreement depended on two things: that suitable Flemish-
speaking subjects should be found, and that sufficient
time should be given her to form them in the image of
Notre Dame. So energetically did he set to work, that
by August 28th of the same year the Foundress was
once more on the road to Flanders to receive the postulants he had recruited for her. Marie Steenhaut—
later to become the first annalist of the Institute—
awaited her at the episcopal palace. On entering the
parish church, Sister Marie recorded later in her
Memoirs, "One of my sisters, whom she did not know
at all, was praying there, and our Mother knelt behind
her. She came out with us, and made acquaintance on
the road. Mère Julie told her that she also would one
day be her daughter, and when I was alone with her she
told me that God had given her special lights on the
future of this child." This little girl, Ciska Steenhaut,
had already been favoured by God. A year before her
meeting with Julie, when praying in the church, "she
suddenly beheld the altar surrounded by a dazzling
light, and heard a voice distinctly say to her: 'Be faithful to Me, you will be a religious.'" Both at the time
of this occurrence and at that of the meeting with Julie,
Ciska had no intention of entering the Religious Life.
A year later, when Julie visited Flanders again, Ciska
stood waiting for her just as her sister had done.

When her work was finished in Ghent, Mère Julie,
accompanied by Marie Steenhaut, went on to Courtrai.
Here the Foundress met and embraced Thérèse
Goethals, a child of six, who would grow up to be the
third Superior General of Notre Dame, and the first to
send the Sisters to America. The formation of Sister
Marie Steenhaut began on this journey. She had a
young lady's vanity and horror of appearing ridiculous,
and, to exercise her in humility, Mère Julie mortified
her in these things.

"She made me sit down at the stall of a woman who was selling fruit, and bought from her some pears, which she told me to eat with the bread she took out of her bag," records Sister Marie. "To eat thus in the street was my first humiliation. I kept fancying that among the passers-by were persons come from Ghent to the Fair then going on at Courtrai. Next day our Mother took me to High Mass, and on the way she was more than once jeered at by the boys on account of her somewhat singular travelling costume; they greeted her as 'witch,' 'black sorceress,' etc. She made me translate these titles into French for her, and laughed heartily over them. Not so I; indeed, so humbled did I feel, that when we entered the church I let her go on in front and knelt at a distance from her. She took no notice of this till we were leaving the church, when she asked me my reason. I confessed my pride, and she was pleased with my sincerity; but she spoke to me about humility in a way which deepened my esteem for her, and I was stronger in the subsequent tests to which she put me."

There is a lovely intimacy about passages like these, and they give a very good idea of what the early Sisters meant when they said that their Mother led them "with great gentleness, like the children of a family." To a Mother there is no such thing as a comprehensive unit called "the family": there are children, each to be loved and watched over individually. This is splendidly illustrated in a letter sent to the Amiens community from Flanders, which, because it is the most beautiful of all her letters, deserves to be quoted in full in any work on Julie Billiart. She writes:

"I wish you all those things which will best please the heart of our good Jesus: that you may all become faithful servants of that Lord to whom we are consecrated. Our body, our soul, our mind, everything in us ought *to be Jesus*. Oh, my daughters, how sweet it is to die every moment to our own life so as to let only the spirit of our loving Jesus live in us.

"But the life of Jesus in us requires that we should all become like Him—gentle, patient, charitable, forbearing. Yes, love Him, my good Sister Sophie; love Him, my good Sister Frances, and with a generous love which breaks through all obstacles; love Him, my good Sister Genevieve, set yourself to work in earnest. Courage, my good little Eulalie, courage; you will see how good the good God is. As for Sister Theresa, she appears to make only material bread; but she knows better; in making it, she is feeding her soul with another food. Sister Firmine is going this year to acquire a simplicity which will be the delight of the adorable Heart of our dear and good Jesus. My good Sister Angélique will now always be with the angels at the foot of the altar. My little Sister Scholastica will grow quite childlike in the company of her little pupils; let her remember to offer them every day to Jesus, Mary and Joseph. And our good Sister Catherine, with all her family, she has a work to do to form Jesus in those young hearts. As for the others, Sisters Clothilde, Marianne, Seraphine, all that have come, all that are to come, may my Jesus ever live in their hearts."

A true Mother's heart beats in that letter: one can picture her spiritual children gathering to read it, and the smile and blush of pleasure that greeted the announcing of each name. Nor was anyone forgotten.

Julie's second visit to Flanders was for the purpose of establishing a house at Saint-Nicolas, near Ghent, in accordance with the suggestion of the Bishop. The premises were known as "den Berkenboom," and, at the time of Julie's arrival, two Sisters of a Philippine Congregation, who had grown old and worn in a heart-breaking effort to keep a school going, were only too pleased to yield place to younger hands. The building was in hopeless repair, the sanitation bad. Mère Julie waited for assurances that these things would be attended to, before she returned to Amiens. She sent a group to begin work there, with Justine Garçon, one of the first four professed, as Superior. Among the group was Marie Steenhaut. The scene of their sending forth has a gospel fragrance about it. The evening of the Immaculate Conception, 1807. On the point of their departure, Julie said the Lord's Prayer slowly over them, and then said: "Holy Father, keep them in

Thy name whom Thou hast given me, that they may be one, as we also are one, and that they may ever remain one with the common centre." Then they stood, and Julie and the rest of the Sisters knelt to kiss their feet, because their feet were of those who set off with the Gospel of Peace, and therefore their feet were beautiful.

Julie accompanied the new community to Ghent, and while there an event of great significance occurred. She received a letter from Monseigneur Pisani de la Gaude, who then governed the diocese of Namur, asking her to found a house in his episcopal city. The Institute of Notre Dame was to become the Institute of Notre Dame of Namur, because in the stormy years ahead, Namur was to be the centre of strength and cohesion. In Charles Francis Joseph Pisani, Baron de la Gaude, the Institute met one of its staunchest supports and warmest friends. His portrait shows a very aristocratic face, suffused with something of a holy kindness. Driven underground by the Revolution, he had succeeded in making his way to Rome, and when the Concordat was signed in 1804, he was appointed Bishop of Namur. For his loyalty to their Institute, Monseigneur Pisani should be held in grateful remembrance by every Sister of Notre Dame.

The account of her journey to Namur is another of those vignettes of sorrow and humiliation of which her life provides so many examples, and which show so clearly the patience and sweetness of her soul. She left Ghent for Namur, we are told, on a bitter day in January, and Mère Blin's account of her arrival is one of the really fine things in her Chronicle:

"Rain and sleet had set in with the fall of darkness. When she had crossed the town, wading in mud, she reached the house of the Bishop of Namur, mud-spattered, soaked, and starving. To increase her discomfort, she was received by a

very ill-humoured servant, who spoke churlishly to her, and
sent her to search for a night's shelter in a town where she was
a complete stranger. He told her that the Bishop was busy,
and that he would not announce her. Our good Mother began
to depart, not knowing where to go, but apparently his good
angel enlightened the uncouth fellow on just what had passed
between Julie and himself in their conversation, so that he
suddenly understood that his Lordship had asked for her and
that she came by his orders, because he called her back, announced her and showed her in to his Master. The Bishop
heaped kindnesses on her, made her lodge with him, and enter-
tained her for three days. All was arranged that she should
return in the summer with some Sisters, and his Lordship lost
no time in renting a house and furnishing it with all neces-
saries."

It is hard to do justice in translation to this passage:
those who read it in the original will not easily forget
the wet and bedraggled Foundress, standing alone and
bewildered on the episcopal doorstep, with sleet stinging her face. "Elle arriva chez Monseigneur de Namur,
crottée, mouillée, gelée. . . ." (She arrived at the
Bishop's House, mud-bespattered, wet through and
perished.)

On the twentieth of the following June, Mère Julie
returned to Namur, to make the foundation that came
to be regarded as the second cradle of Notre Dame.
With her came Mère Blin de Bourdon. It was indeed
fitting that at this important moment in the history of
Notre Dame, these spiritual twin-souls should be found
together. It could serve as an earnest of friendship and
solidarity in the clammy muddle of well-meaning and
doubtfully-motivated stupidity which was soon to en-
velop Mère Julie as a last, great, purifying trial.

MÈRE JULIE RETURNED TO NAMUR

CHAPTER SEVEN

THE CORNER-STONE REJECTED

THERE is a strange and wonderful power in Virginity—that is, in the voluntary consecration of the whole being, body as well as soul, for the love of God. The last words are the operative ones: and St. Paul's warnings in the matter are well known. When we think of virginity as of something white, it should be as the white heat of the love of God. Virginity, too, is thought of as a flower, and that is why, combining the ideas of blossoming and of whiteness, we have placed the lily in the hands of our virgin saints —a strange lily, when we examine our idea of it, since, from many associations with the Canticle and the Litanies, we have endowed it also with the fragrance of the rose. The whole idea of Christian virginity is foreign to the carnal man: he sees it as a bitter, barren soil, or, if he adopts the traditional image, its flower is something exotic and repulsive. "Virginity, austere bloom," wrote Gautier, "born of a soil drenched with blood, whose withered and sickly flower burgeons with many a pang amid the dank shadows of nunneries, beneath chill, cleansing rain; rose without fragrance and bristling without thorns." There is nothing barren in Christian virginity, for it is nothing less than a rich and fertile union with the Godhead, in which all the powers of the soul are focused and intensified, and there results an increase of vital energy. In this energy, a great strength of soul is born, the strength of humility, the strength of meekness, the strength of charity, the strength of Him Who said: "Learn of Me,

95

because I am meek and humble of heart." A convent, then, is not a hiding-place for blighted matrimonial hopes, as it were a heap of dried leaves: much less is it a garden of sickly, consumptive joylessness. Yet Gautier was wiser than he knew when he spoke of virginity as "a soil drenched in blood." The spiritual soil of the human soul is drenched with the Blood of Jesus Christ, and the most perfect flower of humanity— the flower of Christian virginity—is alive and strong with the sap of God. "I live," said St. Paul, "now not I, but Christ liveth in me."

It was necessary thus to locate and examine briefly the beauty and inherent strength of Christian virginity, that the strength of soul, and the source of that strength, which carried Julie Billiart gloriously through a night of petty persecution, may be fully appreciated.

When Père Varin left Amiens, he committed the Sisters of Notre Dame to the care of his colleague, Père Leblanc, and at the same time appointed as their confessor the Abbé de Sambucy de Saint-Estève, who had already filled the same post at the convent of the Ladies of the Sacred Heart in Amiens. At the moment of Julie's departure from Amiens for Namur, a very significant occurrence took place. M. de Sambucy walked a little distance with Julie, then turned to her and said in a tone of finality: "Mère Julie, you have now finished your work here; you must do it elsewhere." The full import of these words was brought home to Julie, when, at Namur, Père Leblanc said sorrowfully to her: "My dear Mother, your influence over affairs in the Amiens house is now as little as my own." For a spirit of indirection, of exaggeration, of semi-hysteria even, had replaced the deep, calm, spiritual common sense of the Foundress in the community of Amiens. Youth was at the helm, and virtues were not virtues unless they had in them what the co-Foundress called "toutes les saillies de la jeunesse" ("all the gush of

youth"). These vagaries of youth were given full reign
because the Bishop of Amiens, Mgr. Demandolx, was
being systematically and deliberately turned against the
Foundress. He was a good and pious man, but of
pendulum-like disposition, inclined to swing from one
extreme to the other, and like all such natures, subject
to great nervous tension. Between these two clerics,
Mgr. Demandolx, already suffering from the brain
disease that was his ultimate fate, and M. de Sambucy,
obsessed by his own unbalanced ideas, the great design
of Notre Dame would certainly have been wrecked, had
not the hand of God been in it.

Notre Dame had been born in one spirit, the spirit
that is perfectly indicated by the early Sisters when they
said that their Mother led them " with great gentleness,
like the children of a family." There was to be no exaggeration, nothing spiritually *recherché*, in this family:
its spirit was to be a spirit of simplicity, and a joy in
obedience and suffering which found its expression in
the saying which had become inseparably associated with
any thought of Julie Billiart: "Oh, how good He is,
the God of goodness." M. de Sambucy attempted to
shape the new Congregation to the model of the ancient
monastic institutes, thereby altering the whole spirit
in which it was conceived. "He would have no
Superior General," we are told, "no connection
between the different houses, no extension of the
Institute beyond the single diocese of Amiens." He was
merely confessor to the community, with very limited
powers, but he seemed quite anxious to act beyond his
powers; and, to further his designs, he attempted to
poison Père Varin against Julie. As yet, however, he
did not succeed in this, and his efforts merely underlined the fact that the Foundress was yielding too much
to him. "Mother," Père Varin often said to her,
"since God has put you in the position you occupy, you
have grace to act; do not tie yourself to asking so many

G

permissions of M. de Sambucy; if you consult him, let
it be as a friend merely. Whatever confidence I may
have in him for other things, it is not to him that I look
to give your daughters the spirit they need to enter
into the designs of Our Lord; and if he is not to give
the spirit, neither is be to preserve or perfect it. No,
that is the task Our Lord has committed to you, Mère
Julie."

It would seem that Père Varin was not altogether
free to remove M. de Sambucy, because the latter was in
high favour with Mgr. Demandolx, Bishop of Amiens.
He had to content himself, as he said in one of his
letters, with giving him several "bits of advice which
were not very flattering to him, but which were intended to establish the rights of the Mother over her
daughters." The "bits of advice" very obviously fell
on shut ears. Even before the web began to be spun
in real earnest, Julie's attitude of simplicity and resignation is apparent. She has no illusions about M. de
Sambucy, but she interprets all with a wealth of charity.
"His intentions are good," she used to say; "leave all
to God. M. de Sambucy has excellent qualities, but he
is not the right man in the right place. Let us humble
ourselves and wait. God holds all the events of life in
His hands, and can make those which, to us, seem the
most vexatious, turn to His greater glory."

"The smouldering displeasure of the confessor first broke
forth on the occasion of Julie's visit to Flanders. His opposition to the foundation of St.-Nicolas was, however, forced to
give way before the authority of his own Superior, Père
Leblanc, nor could he prevent the consequent arrangements
made by the Servant of God for fresh foundations, and for the
regular visitation of the branch houses thus established. But
one thing he successfully did. He managed to prejudice against
her the minds of the ecclesiastical authorities, and on her return
to Amiens she was met with undeserved reproaches and rebukes,
accepted, after the fashion of the saints, in silence."

These words, from one of her biographers, set the pattern of these years in the life of Julie Billiart: first, a sincere effort of hers to promote God's glory, then that effort misjudged and misrepresented, and finally, reproach and even abusive words.

Mère Blin, the co-Foundress, was a stumbling block to M. de Sambucy, for he knew the depth of her friendship for Julie, and the strength that her presence gave. Perhaps he saw something, at times, of the quiet appraisal of the French aristocrat, in glances which escaped the guard of grace, and the vague discomfort these glances caused determined him more than ever to separate the two Foundresses.   Both the foundation at Namur and the list of Sisters for the new community had been approved, and busy preparations for departure on the following day were in progress, when M. de Sambucy arrived with a counter-order, which he had wheedled from the Bishop, appointing Mère Blin Superior in place of the Sister named by the Mother General.   Moreover, he had succeeded in obtaining command of the small capital in hand, derived from a gift and from the sale of some property belonging to Mère Blin: this he handed over to the Ladies of the Sacred Heart as a loan without interest.   Furthermore, he assumed control of Mère Blin's entire income during her absence, and took care to settle it completely on the house at Amiens.   Finally—for M. de Sambucy did nothing by halves—he obtained an order that Mère Julie should not delay at Namur, but should pass on to found a new house at Bordeaux.   Next day, as we have seen, he bade God-speed to the two Sisters: "You have now finished your work here; you must do it elsewhere." Meantime, M. de Sambucy would have a free hand to begin his work in real earnest in Amiens: for, writes Mère Blin, "he took for granted, I know not on what grounds, that Mère Julie's absence would be for months . . . or for years."

Nothing was right: everything must be changed, even the names of the Sisters. M. de Sambucy selected Sister Thérèse, renaming her Mère Victoire, a name which seemed to commemorate the victory of his own ideas, and established her as Superior over the Amiens house. She was twenty-three years old and had been but nineteen months in the community: she had been cook and children's nurse before entering, and she seems to have acquired a little of the polish of the family for whom she worked, sufficient to delude M. de Sambucy into supposing that in her he had found the youthful leader of Notre Dame.

"Of a strong temperament," writes Mère Blin, "she was not without a certain vigour of soul which was useful in checking her too great vivacity, her almost continual emotional out-pourings, in a word, all the gush of youth. She had a good heart, and did not lack memory, or taste, or good dispositions; but her humility was weak, since she had not been exercised in the acts which form that virtue, and how could she, there-fore, without prejudice to her soul, sustain the eulogies and expressions of admiration which came on her like rain. She did not lack judgment, and she had some appreciation of the dangers to which she was exposed: she wished to resist the order appointing her as Superior, it even caused her to fall ill, but she had to yield. I know not what spirit was then reigning, that the superiors, even many of the townspeople and the whole community, with few exceptions, admired and praised her pro-fusely."

From the beginning, the whole affair seems to have been unfortunate. Even her reluctance to accept office was but a travesty of the real reluctance of the saints, arising from humility and the fear of God, not incom-patible with a knowledge of their own ability, and serving to confirm superiors as to the wisdom of their choice. Here was the genuine fear of the inexperienced and uneducated before a task they recognize to be beyond their powers, and it is certainly no tribute to the spiritual knowledge of M. de Sambucy that he failed to appreciate the real source of this fear, or the significance of its speedy disappearance in the sunshine of human praise.

No sooner had Mère Victoire taken charge of the house in Amiens than the atmosphere became charged with noisy and unhealthy affection in the community and extended to dangerous exaggerations in penance and in prayer. Had Notre Dame been left long in the way on which M. de Sambucy had placed it, it would have ceased after a short, hectic fever. The symptoms are all present in Mère Blin's account of the relations between the Sisters and their new Superior. She writes:

" Monsieur de Sambucy consulted her and sent people to her for spiritual direction. Some of the young Sisters, who discovered in her a sympathy with that instinct in their nature to attach themselves, clung to her with all the sentimentality of their adolescence. Some cut off pieces of her hair, others kissed her habit, and at recreation, now become a noisy affair, nearly all surrounded her, pressed close about her, and were happy only if they succeeded in touching her: they vied with each other in glorifying her with the name of saint and penitent. She scarcely ate, perhaps from a desire for mortification, but also from natural caprice, as is often the case with people who suffer from bad nerves, as she indeed greatly suffered. The young Sisters, who saw this abstinence of their Mother, thought it a holy and a wholesome thing to leave off eating when they had scarcely satisfied half their appetite, because perfection consisted in this; and if this madness had continued long, they would have destroyed their capacity for the work to which they were called, a work demanding robust health. What in particular was extremely hurtful to Mère Victoire, both as to soul and body, was that M. de Sambucy made her spend three or four hours in prayer every day, and forbade her to take part in those household tasks which would have provided the exercise so necessary for one of her temperament, and which Mère Julie was always so careful to provide for her. In this, he believed that he was acting for the best, and it is not to be wondered at that his youth and his complete lack of experience caused him to be deceived in many things."

No wonder, too, that with such lack of experience in
mind, Mère Julie should have given as her considered
opinion that a young director in a community of nuns
was "an unfortunate necessity" ("une fâcheuse néces-
sité"): and does not the aristocrat look out for a brief
second from the pages of Mère Blin's manuscript, in a
phrase redolent of her brilliant débutante days, when
she writes in the context of all this youthful gush:
"Les hommes ne sont pas universels" ("Men are not
all-capable! ").

That M. de Sambucy was far from being all-capable,
is very evident in the rest of this unfortunate affair.   In
fact, a biographer who attempts to seek motives in the
muddle is surprised by many things.   Père Varin, as we
have seen, advised Julie to be careful not to defer to
M. de Sambucy except as a friend: and at the same time
he writes to the confessor: "Watch the principal steps
taken by Mère Julie, and give me an account of them."
The safest comment we can allow ourselves on all this
is that of Mère Blin.   "From all this," she says, "there
resulted many things badly undertaken and badly
interpreted . . . and badly rendered, which were
a source of much mortification to our Mère Julie
and which God, as a good Father, husbanded for
her."

Meantime, M. de Sambucy had seized all correspondence to and from Mère Julie at Amiens. For several
months she received no news of her spiritual children
there, and she was a prey to great anxiety.   "Mère
Julie," writes Mère Blin, who was in constant com-
munication with her at that time, "suffered extremely
from this silence, and even more from a certain secret
urge which ceaselessly called her back to Amiens and
caused her great uneasiness."   Even the love and devotion of the Sisters in Bordeaux were powerless to keep
her thoughts from Amiens.   In contrast to her rejection
in Amiens, the Archbishop of Bordeaux held her in

great esteem, treated her with kindness, and received her formally under the title "Mother General." The harvest of Notre Dame in Bordeaux was a rich one. On September 8th, 1807, the Archbishop gave the veil and habit to eighteen new members: a second house of formation was opened in the city, and the number of children in each house grew to seven hundred. Still the months went by, and every day of those months was marked by a great anxiety for her daughters in Amiens. Why was there no word from them? . . . What was happening? . . . Then one day a letter, written in a very paternal fashion, arrived from the Bishop of Amiens, asking Julie to return. She also received the letter we have already quoted, from Monsieur Varin. In great joy at the prospect of meeting her dear daughters again, she left Bordeaux for Amiens on November 12th, 1807.

Her journey was an arid and coldly friendless one, for M. de Sambucy had been tireless in spreading tales which closed, as with a block of ice, hearts that had been warmly flung wide to her at every stage of her journey to Bordeaux some months earlier. She rested for a while with the Ladies of the Sacred Heart at Poitiers, and even began a retreat there, but inter-rupted it because of a tremendous anxiety urging her to press on. Madame Barat, Superior General of the "Ladies" and so lately her good friend, had received her frigidly. Bewildered, but trusting with great sim-plicity in God, she continued on her way, a way in which she was to meet with nothing but "ice and storms," as Mère Blin remarks. On November 20th she arrived at Paris, and stopped at the house of her friend, Madame Leclercq. She immediately hastened to the great house of the Sisters of Charity, where she had received such a warm welcome on her passage to Bordeaux, and whose Superior General had been her guest at Amiens, so that Julie had conceived a great personal regard and affection for her. She hastened, then, as one does to where a warmth of kindness and affection is expected: joyfully, careless of ceremony, eager to open the door and just walk in: but the icy chill from Amiens had reached the convent before her, and she found no warmth there. Tone, manner, all was changed, and the Superior General stood erect and frigid before her in icy reception. Utterly bewildered now and deeply hurt, Julie humbly waited. There was a moment's silence. Then the Superior General drew a letter from her pocket and handed it to Julie. It was from the Bishop of Amiens, the ink of whose paternal invitation was scarcely dry, forbidding Julie to cross the threshold of the Faubourg house, or even to enter the diocese of Amiens. . . . In a matter of days, the great pendulum of Mgr. Demandolx's moods had swung completely out of her favour, and M. de Sambucy once again had his way.

Deeply distressed, the thought of M. Varin remained with her as a ray of light in the pathless murk which had suddenly come about her. With him, all would be clear; he would explain everything, he would console her. But she was bringing her desolation to a wilderness of desolation, her bewilderment to a man bewildered. Before seeking him, she had spent two hours prostrate in prayer before the Blessed Sacrament, and it was well that she should have done so, that grace might be given her to bear the unkindest cut of all. Julie was completely unaware of the Toussaint decree of Napoleon ordering the dispersion of the Fathers of the Faith and the dissolution of their colleges. Even in the midst of this disaster, M. de Sambucy did not cease to pour out complaints to Père Varin about Mère Julie—complaints which registered as crimes in the atmosphere of disappointment, distress and shattered nerves in which they were heard. M. de Sambucy was not a bad man, but simply an example of the good man with one blind spot, with one obsession, the obsession which made him work towards the expulsion of Julie from the Amiens house, in the firm conviction that the glory of God lay in the implementing of his ideas, of his plans for Notre Dame. His conduct with regard to Julie can only be interpreted as that strange aberration which can even see the Will of God in the vagaries of self-will. In pursuance of his campaign against Julie, he was at that very moment in Paris, and when the news reached him of her return from Bordeaux, he said in an angry voice: *"Elle a donc fait son coup!"* ("She has played her cards, then!"). Again M. de Sambucy had succeeded, for M. Varin received Julie with harsh words and heaped-up accusations.

What was the source of all this pother? When the accusations are examined, in so far as at this stage we can gather anything specific, they are found to be so petty as to be utterly unworthy of rational men. For example, there was the affair of the vestments. . . . "M. de Sambucy was not the only instrument of which God made use to procure the disgrace of Mère Julie in the eyes of his Lordship the Bishop of Amiens. One of the Fathers of the Faith served this purpose very well. He was scrupulous and had few talents, and therefore M. Varin appointed him our chaplain" (Mère Blin). This priest remained about a year in this office, and received all respect and attention. Mère Blin, however, had no illusions about him.

"It was easily gathered," she writes, "that differences of character and of disposition left no room for sympathy between this priest and Julie: in a word, this good man saw Mère Julie through prejudiced eyes. He was an old friend of the Bishop, and when Julie Billiart was discussed at the dining table, he lost no opportunity of painting her character in the colours of his own prejudiced vision. He often succeeded in insinuating his own false ideas into the Bishop's mind . . . and from thence they were carried to M. de Sambucy, who gathered them

all together and passed them in turn to M. Varin, who made
them his material for accusation and lecture when she sought
his encouragement and help in a cold and cheerless hour."

We shall examine more closely one such accusation,
passed industriously along this chain of prejudice,
assuming ever greater proportions of wickedness as it is
sifted and analysed and held up at different angles.

She was accused of having refused to give certain
vestments to the chaplain. For those who have an ear
for undertones in prose, there is an admirable restraint
and patience in Mère Blin's account.

" We had in the house," she writes, " a very beautiful, hand-
embroidered chasuble, belonging to M. Thomas. He lent it
only on condition that it should be well looked after. Con-
sequently, without foreseeing that he might ask for it, our
Mother told the sacristan not to give it to the chaplain—that
is, not to offer it to him. However, he asked for it just before
beginning Mass, and the sacristan tactlessly told him that our
Mother had forbidden her to give it to him, which was not the
case at all since she did not tell her to refuse it to him. Occur-
rences of this kind," she comments, " appear monstrous when
painted in prejudiced colours."

Trifles light as air can certainly become confirmations
strong as proofs of Holy Writ, when a fact looks to the
eye, as the eye likes the look. . . .

With the catalogue of her failings still ringing in
her ears, Mère Julie made her bewildered way back to
the house of Madame Leclercq. This good lady wrote
to the Curé of Amiens Cathedral, begging him to inter-
cede with the Bishop in order to obtain permission for
Julie to go to St. Just to a priest she had known for many
years, M. de Lamarche. Permission was given, but
when she arrived in St. Just, M. de Lamarche was not
at home. After mature consideration, and being now
completely worn out, she decided to continue to
Amiens, where she was warmly welcomed by Madame

de Rumigny. She remained two days with her, while
steps were taken to discover from the Bishop what precisely were the accusations against her, and whether
there was anything she could do about them. Meantime, in the house of Madame de Rumigny, a strange
frightening occurrence took place. It was as though
Julie were allowed to see, hideously embodied and
standing in the room before her, the diabolical opposition of hell to her work for souls. That this symbol
should be the expression on the face of a Religious gives
the whole occurrence a unique thrill of horror. Mère
Blin records the incident in detail.

"Meantime," she writes, "I cannot pass over in silence a
circumstance of her stay with Madame de Rumigny. It will
prove how much everyone who had any relations with M. de
Sambucy became imbued with his own prejudices against his
Foundress. At the dispersion of the Fathers of the Faith, one
of the Brothers, named Leonard, had attached himself to the
service of the Abbé de Sambucy; he became his attendant and
messenger. Accordingly, he came to Madame de Rumigny's
house when our Mother was there, and M. Bicheron, a good
priest who lodged in the same house, was present, with Madame
de Rumigny, M. Cotu and M. le Curé de la Cathédrale. Our
Mother has since told me that no words could describe
Leonard's face when he saw her. In an extraordinary voice,
he shouted: 'You are very wrong to have returned!' 'I did
not do so without taking counsel,' she answered. M. Bicheron,
a strong and robust man in perfect health, glanced at Leonard,
and was almost on the instant violently and unaccountably
sick, so that a doctor had to be sent for. . . . When he improved a little, Mère Julie asked him: 'What is the matter
with you? How did this come on?' 'It was Leonard's face,'
he answered. 'Did you not see Leonard's face?'"

It would be interesting to speculate on this strange
occurrence, but perhaps it is wiser to leave it to rest
in Mère Blin's comment: "In all the strange circumstances in which Mère Julie found herself, she gave
homage to God, and thought no more about it."

Immediately after this, Mère Julie wrote to the Bishop of Amiens begging for his goodwill, and for forgiveness of faults, the nature of which she could by no means discover. His reply was merely an urgent wish that she should depart for Namur. Weakness and worn-down health made this impossible for her, and she again requested leave to enter the house of the Faubourg Noyon. After a short delay, this was granted to her.

Several things had combined to set the pendulum moving again in her favour. Mère Victoire had taken on herself to give instruction to the Sisters, in the manner of Mère Julie, and she was proving hopelessly incompetent. Several priests had urged this fact on the Bishop, and the solution he had suggested was one which was displeasing both to the Sisters and to M. de Sambucy, for he proposed putting an Ursuline in Mère Victoire's place as Superior of the Amiens house. It was at this stage that Mère Julie returned—"a poor, unminded outlaw sneaking home." She went up to her room by a little back stairs, quietly, "incognito, like a criminal," says Mère Blin—and, because she was exhausted from the burden of many sufferings, she went immediately to bed.

Almost at once, the whisper went about that Mère Julie had returned. Singly and in little groups they began to come to her, and among the first to do so was Mère Victoire herself. "She surrendered the keys of the house to her," says Mère Blin, "and characteristically gave a tremendous display of affection and attachment": then, leaving the room, she said to the Sisters, "I am still Superior: if you have any difficulties, come to me." To her intimates, she confided that M. de Sambucy had told her that, when Mère Julie returned, she should hand over the keys as a mark of respect, but that she herself should remain Superior. It is obvious that the fear of having an Ursuline placed over her, and

the hurt to her pride in the danger of her being removed
from office, had unnerved her, so that, in a moment of
supreme importance for her, she behaves like the unbalanced, adolescent type she always was : she is excited,
nervous, jumpy. M. de Sambucy said that, for his part,
Mère Julie could return—indeed, he had no option in
the matter : but she would not be Superior of the house.
The Bishop, however, very definitely would no longer
have Mère Victoire in that office, and therefore it was
necessary to withdraw her with all possible grace and
dignity. Torn between conflicting emotions of dogged-
ness, hurt pride, and fear, Mère Victoire became ill,
and remained in bed for several weeks, just at the time
when Mère Julie was gaining health and strength very
rapidly. Meantime, as a further saving of face, M. de
Sambucy was replaced by M. Cottu—an apparent
change only in the state of affairs, since M. Cottu lived
with M. de Sambucy, consulted him in all things, and
rigidly followed his instructions. " It is the wish of
M. de Sambucy that . . ." " M. de Sambucy does not
see his way to . . ." such were the inevitable introduc-
tions to decisions on all matters. M. de Sambucy was
still in control, and he communicated his prejudices
against the Foundress to his successor, who very
soon abandoned his paternal attitude, and became a
perfect successor to the moods of M. de Sambucy.
The campaign against Julie was to go on without
respite.

Everything that Mère Julie did was keenly scrutin-
ized, and at the very best, was found to be lacking in
proper deference to authority : while everything con-
nected with Mère Victoire had the grace and perfection
of an angel, whose very dreaming—" for," says Mère
Blin, " she often dreamed aloud "—was to be received
with awe and reverence. " In fine," writes Mère Blin,
" many times, both in writing and speaking, he heaped
invectives on Mère Julie. She was jealous as a tiger,

she sought to humiliate Mère Victoire at every opportunity, to make a martyr of her: but the more your
pride seeks to humiliate her, he says, so much the more
will her virtue triumph; for you have neither humility
nor charity nor obedience, etc., etc." It was indeed a
duet of praise-singing and invective-pouring: for the
Bishop of Amiens listened to all, joined in the praise
of an "angel" he did not even know, and in the be-
littling of an angel he had not the grace to recognize.
Nevertheless, in the state of affairs at Amiens, he had
no option but to appoint Mère Julie as Superior, but
by appointing Mère Victoire as Assistant, he left
matters in as great a chaos as before.

In this new position, Mère Victoire was keenly sensitive to the least lack of respect in any of the Sisters,
or to a slight act of forgetfulness on the part of Mère
Julie: and in spite of a great lip-humility and submission, she poured out petulant complaints to M. de Cottu
and M. de Sambucy, the latter now being extraordinary
confessor to the community. The relations between
Mère Julie and Mère Victoire are clearly indicated by
the annalist. "It can be said," she writes, "that the
heart of Mère Julie was ever open to her, that she spoke
to her with confidence, treated her with friendship,
regard and consideration; but she could not give her
her full confidence, because she did not consider her
capable of forming the Sister novices, but rather of
injuring them by her dissipation and her lack of
experience." The position as thus analysed was an
extremely delicate one: a Superior with an Assistant
who saw insult and slight in the most innocent of
actions, when coloured by her own hectic imagination;
an Assistant, moreover, whose angelic reputation gave
her the ear of the highest Ecclesiastic powers in Amiens,
eager to listen to her litany of petty complaints. The
conspiracy between M. de Sambucy and M. Cottu to
render null the power of Mère Julie was intensified;

so that, in the words of the annalist, "she became, not a Superior, but merely a person appointed to teach the catechism." Apart altogether from the influence of M. de Sambucy on him, M. de Cottu was himself of a touchy nature which the least contradiction would cause to blaze out, so that, notes Mère Blin, "he was often seen in such a violent temper with Mère Julie as to make one sigh for human feebleness. On such occasions," she goes on, "our poor Mother was intimidated and would not dare to offer an explanation. Every visit of M. Cottu to the house would set the Sisters trembling in sympathy with their Mother." On one occasion, his language to her was so outrageous that he later felt himself bound to offer an apology before the Sisters who had been present, and this caused greater embarrassment to her humility than any hard words or reproaches.

Shortly after this a whirlwind again struck Mère Julie, this time with M. de Sambucy as prime mover. Even the ubiquitous charity of the annalist cannot exonerate M. de Sambucy from deliberate misrepresentation of this incident, since the kindness of the Foundress to her children was as established a fact as the fact of her own existence. The Sisters were unanimous in asserting that Mère Julie watched carefully over the use of the discipline by her daughters, "since, being young and destined for hard apostolic work, prudence and the advice of enlightened minds gave her a great reserve in this matter." However, on one occasion and for a special reason, she allowed a Sister to use the discipline in a very definite and limited way. During her absence, however, the exaggerated zeal of the Sister caused her to take the discipline unto blood. When M. de Sambucy visited the house, he heard of it, questioned the Sister, drew up a document of accusation against the Foundress, which he somehow persuaded the Sister to sign, and forwarded it to the Bishop as an example of her constant inhumanity in her treatment of the Sisters.

The long list of petty jealousy and stupid opposition is far from complete: but it is useful to pause at this stage that we may admire the beauty and simplicity of Julie Billiart. "Mère Julie will be canonized some day," said Mgr. Pisani, who had seen the wonder of her patience, "because during all her long trials at Amiens she never once failed in charity." Every great and chosen soul must pass through its swarms of gadflies, and when that soul is the sensitive soul of a woman, the swarm of gadflies has a power to sting and hurt: but the endurance of such a soul is equal to the buzz and sting of petty persecution because the eye is single and the whole being is lightsome. Hell and the subtlety of Hell is powerless against the child-like simplicity, which Christ made the *sine qua non* of entry into heaven: the child-like simplicity which takes the Fatherhood of God with a magnificent literalness, and passes, by means of the crosses of life, to rest in the Heart of Christ. When heavy storm-clouds were thickest, she wrote to Mère Blin:

"How much we shall have to say to each other, dear friend, when it pleases the Divine Goodness to let us meet! Ah, yes! much that I have laid down in the sweet and loving Heart of Jesus—otherwise I could not have borne the burden. It was heavy enough to kill ten poor Julies like me. I am worth nothing at all for heaven yet. Do pray that the various trials it pleases Our Lord to send me may serve to sanctify me. I am so clumsy, I make a mess of everything. . . . But courage! let us not ask for rest yet. No, no, time presses and the day is far spent. Let us set no bounds to our generosity towards the good God, and He will be lavish towards us."

An extract like that uncovers, as perfectly as possible, the hidden strength that saved Notre Dame: the strength of simplicity, of humility, of trust, the strength that is strong in the knowledge of its own weakness,

save in its *grappling of the soul to God*—to use Mère
Julie's vivid phrase. "This is my one prayer," she
writes. "My Jesus, fasten me tight to Thy Blessed
Cross, and hold me there, for I am nothing but misery.
. . . My heart and my soul rest in God, in spite of the
fogs."

The fogs had indeed been thick about her, cold and
clammy and opaque with short-sighted judgments and
stupid misrepresentations. But she walked steadily in
the light of her own simplicity, and in the end, the
spiritual wedding-garment with which she met the
Bridegroom of her soul, was unspotted by the least
anger or resentful word, because it was woven in perfect
simplicity and the charity of Christ. The lamp of her
charity was always alight, and the murk through which
she was passing was full of the echoes of her song of
praise: "Oh, how good He is, the God of Goodness!"

When the murk had passed, that cry remained as the
motto and inspiration of her followers through centuries, because it lifted up, as it were in a blazing point
of life, the soul of Notre Dame.

H

CHAPTER EIGHT

A TANGLED SKEIN

AN invitation had come to Mère Julie to establish a community of her sisters in Jumet. Three months had passed in exchange of letters between the Bishop of Tournai and the Bishop of Amiens. Now all things were settled, and Mère Julie was asked to name the Sister best suited to begin the new foundation. She immediately named Sœur Victoire—"not," the chronicler hastens to add, "because she considered her to be eminently suited, but because she hoped that in a small house she could live more calmly and have greater opportunity for self-formation, so that the change of place would be beneficial to her." The Mistress of Novices in Amiens was the only alternative, but Julie considered that her removal from this office would be a very great loss to the community. At first the Bishop accepted the nomination with equanimity, but not for long. Whispers were thickly about him: whispers of "tigerish jealousy," "pride," "spitefulness," "wronged angel" and the rest. He decided that things should be done his way, and not according to the dictates of a woman's spite.

It was natural that Mère Julie should have wished to visit in advance those places where her children were to live and work. In the case of Jumet, however, the Bishop, influenced by the whisper of "gadder" recently added to the list and, no doubt, by a certain apprehension as to the result of Mère Julie and Mère Blin coming together in Namur, forbade the Foundress to make the journey, alleging a feeble excuse about unnecessary expense. Moreover, he cancelled the appointment of Sœur Victoire and named the Novice Mistress, Sœur Anastasie Leleu, in her place—a hard decision for Mère Julie, since it deprived her of one of her greatest sources of consolation in all her distress.

"They believed at Amiens," says the chronicler, with a hint of dryness, "that the matter was quite a simple one, that it sufficed merely to send the Sisters; for a spirit of disintegration breathed from all sides." The picture of the arrival of these Sisters into a strange town is a cold and cheerless one. "They found on arrival," the chronicler says, "three sheets, four or five towels, some little bowls and the rest in proportion." There is a hint of great disappointment and heart-soreness in this precise counting of the completely inadequate furnishings of the house, but we are assured that the good Sisters, in the first fine flush of their zeal, reaped great spiritual benefit from their trials. Monsieur le Curé and several others came to their relief, but for a long time it was quite evident things would be in a muddle at Jumet. The whole outcome made apparent the short-sighted policy—or economy—of the Bishop of Amiens in not allowing the Foundress to make a previous visit of inspection. News of the muddle reached him, and he sent for Mère Julie.

To her astonishment, he received her in a friendly manner. Was she content with affairs at Jumet, he asked. "Not at all, your Lordship," she answered, "I am not content either," he said, and then added with a smile, "I give you eight or nine days." No mention of Namur was made, and she concluded that there was nothing to prevent her visiting her daughters there. We are told that Julie, "astonished at such an unexpected change in the Bishop's attitude, saw the finger of God here, and fearing a change of decision, hastened to the coach to secure her place for the morrow." These simple words are an adequate comment on the variabil-

ity of the Bishop's moods.   Even the finger of God, it
would seem, was not to be trusted to remain long
in it!

At Namur, Julie found her three daughters—Mère
Blin, Sœur Xavier and Sœur Gonzague—worn out
with toil and anxiety.   To find her Sisters in this condition must have been a sore trial to the motherly heart
of Mère Julie.   The title "temporal Foundress" has
been given to Mère Blin, for it was with the help of her
money that the Institute was begun.   On this occasion,
much of the conversation between the two Foundresses
was taken up with matters concerning Mère Blin's
income, and especially with a recent transaction in
Amiens.   Monsieur Minsart, their spiritual father, was
also included in these talks.   As a result, it was decided
that Mère Blin should return to Amiens with Mère
Julie for fifteen days.   Thus it came about that a
decision, dictated by a matter of business, was to have
far-reaching effects on the whole subsequent history of
Notre Dame.   She left the conduct of affairs at Namur
in the hands of Sœur Xavier, whose health was already
shattered.   The fifteen days absence became in reality
ten long and eventful months, and when Mère
Blin returned to Namur it was to comfort the last
hours of this Sister of twenty-three.   The early
years of Notre Dame are made lovely by souls like
hers.

At St.-Nicolas where Mère Julie and Mère Blin called
on their way to Amiens, another distressing sight
awaited them.   When the Foundress had sent Sœur St.
Jean as Superior to St.-Nicolas, it was as a healthy woman
in her twenties, "a woman," says the chronicle, "mature
beyond her years, and capable of prudently guiding her
little family."   A ghost of the woman they knew met
them at the door—pale, emaciated, worn out by loss
of sleep, loss of appetite, and by a disease which tortured every part of her body.   The appalling damp-

ness of the house had destroyed her once robust health, as surely as it had blotched and destroyed the walls about her. Utterly distressed, Julie left St.-Nicolas, having promised to send Sœur Catherine Daullée of Montdidier to replace Sœur St. Jean so that she could return to Amiens in an attempt to save her shattered health. A petition for another house had been sent to the minister a year before, but it had lain unanswered in official archives. Always a realist, Julie spent her two days in St.-Nicolas searching for another house, and she succeeded in renting one for a year. Very soon we find her in Paris, moving from one official to another, and obtaining nothing but empty promises. "The only fruits of those Paris journeys," remarks Mère Blin, "were fruits of humility and patience, calculated to prepare her for one of her most trying scenes with Père Varin, arising from the heaped-up accusations industriously forwarded from Amiens by Monsieur de Sambucy." A series of unpleasant events led up to this.

We return for a moment to the smiling face of the Bishop of Amiens as he sends Julie on her journey to Jumet, and we hear his words, friendly, warm, anxious even, as set down on record in the archives: "You will go to Jumet. If your Sisters are in distress there, bring them back to me, and those of St.-Nicolas as well. I do not wish them to die. . . . It is a mortal sin to send them to such a damp house." What was her amazement, therefore, a few days later when, worn out with anxiety for her Sisters, the following letter reached her, forwarded from Jumet.

"His Lordship the Bishop of Amiens to Mère Julie.
"I had already remarked, my dear daughter, that nothing was able to bring you back to that spirit of simplicity and obedience which I had so much recommended to you, and that, in spite of my counsels and your promises, you act, whenever you think my eye is not on you, according to your private

notions and petty personal passions. I am quite able to detect these through the mask of your protestations and sham humility; and I have now fresh proof of them in the audacity with which, on setting out for Jumet, you took on yourself to violate one of the most vital articles of your Rule. It is there stated that in the case of absence of the first Superior, she is to be replaced by the Assistant to whom the Sisters shall render obedience. Yet you have set aside Mère Victoire, and have given orders on your own private authority that, in any difficulty that arises, the Sisters are to address themselves to the Mistress of Novices. Whence can proceed this recommendation of yours, if not from that jealousy which you nourish in the depths of your soul against a subject whom you dislike because she is worth more than yourself, and on whom God will be pleased to shower His graces in proportion as you strive to humble her? I beg to inform you, therefore, that I have re-established things in the condition in which you ought to have left them."

The dry and stony places of anxiety, worry and footsore, fruitless journeyings, were quite sufficient, without a storm from his Grace of Amiens. The fable of the wronged angel and the jealous tiger was already wearing very thin, and once again the whole business is unworthy of rational men. Mère Victoire was a young Nun, inexperienced, unbalanced, a radiating centre of dissipation. Sœur Anastasie had been replaced in the office of Mistress of Novices by Sœur Jeanne Godelle, a woman of excellent judgment, of superior and finished education, and especially of deep faith and sure prudence. When on the point of leaving Amiens, Julie was approached by some of the Sisters with the question: "To whom shall we turn for some spiritual advice in your absence?" Mère Julie immediately and quite simply named the Sister for whose virtues she herself had a deep admiration. There is a hint in this letter of a troubled state of affairs at Amiens, a hint of the coming storm that was to end with the expulsion of the Sisters of Notre Dame from Amiens. It was a hard and bitter letter, enough to try the patience of a saint,

and the saintly patience was there to be tried. Listen
to the comment of the Chronicle:

"It is almost beyond belief how much these frequent changes
of face and manner of acting, which she met with in the most
virtuous people, served to detach her from all things, and to
teach her, by the hard way of experience, that God alone never
changes."

To watch a soul like that of Julie Billiart in a
tempest of pettiness and misunderstanding is to know,
in all its blinding reality, the mystery of the indwelling
of God in the pure soul: for as one watches for the
movement of anger, the quick word, the curt gesture,
here comes instead a mighty brightening in eyes lifted
to God, and an upsurge of hope, of trust, of confidence
that keeps a centre of calm in the midst of the storm.
And the Godhead dwelt in that calm.

On May 5th, 1808, Mère Julie and Mère Blin
reached Amiens, to the intense joy of the Sisters there.
When the first transports of joy on her behalf had spent
themselves, Mère Blin broke the news gently to them
that her visit was to be but a short one. However, as
cares and worries seemed to multiply about her, Mère
Julie arranged that she should stay with her for some
months that together they might meet and seek a solution for problems which were threatening the very
spiritual foundations of their movement. These problems centred around the form which the final draft of
the Constitutions of Notre Dame was to take.

The Fathers of the Faith, says the Chronicle, "had
already thrown some ideas together on a sheet of paper,
which had been presented to the Bishops in whose
dioceses the Sisters had been established." But this state
of affairs was unstable and unsatisfactory both to the
Foundresses and to the Bishop of Amiens. The situation was a delicate one, however, and both the Mothers
held back, pleading that the time was not ripe, and in

reality fearing that the mind of the Bishop was not in harmony with the primitive spirit of Notre Dame. The two cardinal points of his plan were that there should be no Mother General, and that the Institute should not extend beyond the limits of the Diocese of Amiens, a decision which would mean Julie abandoning those Sisters she had already placed in other dioceses. These ideas were conveyed to the Mothers through Monsieur Cottu, now Superior and Confessor of the Amiens house, together with his Lordship's view that Mère Julie's travels were an unnecessary extravagance. Discussion began in the rather glacial atmosphere created by the Bishop's refusal to receive the Mothers on their arrival at Amiens.

Mère Julie and Mère Blin made their point of view so clear to Monsieur Cottu, that he invited Mère Blin to put their ideas on paper. The Mothers consulted together and covered a great deal of paper, but, in the end, the solid peasant common sense of Julie made her see that all this would merely have the effect of sharpening and concentrating the opposition to the primitive spirit of Notre Dame, and so the draft was never given to the Bishop. Mère Blin had, on several occasions, spoken plainly to Monsieur Cottu about the strange attitude of M. de Sambucy towards Mère Julie, and especially in the matter of a series of accusations he had sent to the Bishop of Namur, in an attempt to poison his mind against her. Monsieur Cottu had listened quietly, and then had gone on to make some grudging concessions to Mère Julie's worth, which served to show how deep-dyed he was in the ideas of M. de Sambucy. Mère Blin had been held in great esteem by the Bishop of Namur, whose letter at this time shows his anxiety to have her back : but in Amiens she was regarded with disdain, so that, as she writes of herself, "being of one mind and one heart with Mère Julie, being 'two heads under one veil,' to use the words of the Bishop of Amiens, she drank of the chalice of ignominy held to the lips of her friend."

Meanwhile, the plight of Sœur St. Jean of St.-Nicolas was not forgotten. Mère Julie pointed out to Monsieur Cottu the necessity for recalling her to Amiens, a measure with which he was in full agreement. When Sœur St. Jean returned to Amiens, she was put into the hands of the best doctors, and for a time she appeared to improve. But consumption had found its withering way into her lungs, and it was soon apparent that nothing could be done to save her. She developed that craving, so pathetically characteristic of the doomed consumptive, for the one thing she thought could save her: if she could fill her lungs with the strong air of her own countryside, twelve leagues from Amiens, she would lose that cough that tore her with sharp, dry claws, and she would be well again. Julie hesitated, for she feared an illusion of the devil, but soon yielded to medical advice. Still a Sister of Notre Dame, Sœur St. Jean returned to her parents. Very shortly after this, she was dead.

"I count this a grace which God gave to the good Sister," writes Mère Blin, "for had she continued to live with us, she would have been a witness to all that happened and would have seen the way in which her Mothers were set aside, in the last months of her life. By a mercy of God, she was not involved in the dissolution of the Amiens house, for it would have been an added agony to her sensitive and loyal soul."

She had given a striking proof of this sensitive loyalty in her intercourse with the Bishop of Ghent when she was Superior of St.-Nicolas. The Bishop had studied in the same college as M. de Sambucy. They were, therefore, intimate friends, and M. de Sambucy lost no opportunity of pouring out his grievances against Mère Julie. The Bishop visited the Convent and " in the presence of Monsieur le Doyen and other important persons, said extremely vehement things

against Mère Julie to Sœur St. Jean, ending with:
Your Mother is a gadder whose house must perish,
and if you do not separate yourself from her, you
will perish with her.' Sœur St. Jean refuted these
calumnies with so much prudence and sweetness that
the Bishop began to sing her praises. Her response to
the praises was: 'If the Mother were bad, how could
the daughters be good?'" The simple appeal of this
transparently virtuous religious to the analogy of the
fruit and the tree was staggering, and the Bishop mur-
mured shamefacedly "I am only repeating what I have
been told about her." His comment to Mère Julie
when he heard of Sœur St. Jean's death was: "You
have lost a charming daughter. . . . Oh, what a loss
you have suffered!" And yet, loss is not quite exact:
for it was necessary that the dawn of Notre Dame
should be filled with the good odour of victims chosen
by God for their innocence and loyalty, that the dew
of benediction might be dropped abundantly down.
Souls like Sœur St. Jean and Sœur Xavier are the
brilliancies of that dawn, which merge even as we
wonder at their beauty, but whose emerging will be
found in the day-strength of noon.

Worries of finance and of administration continued
to crowd about the Foundresses. Mère Blin had requested Monsieur Minsart to seek for a bigger house
with a more spacious garden in Namur. He had
searched diligently for months, had found a suitable
place, and then it looked very much as though the
money was not there to meet the purchase. The Bishop
of Amiens was growing impatient at Mère Blin's continued presence in the Amiens house. Mère Julie
pointed out to him that her companion's revenue was
not enough to support both houses, and since her
revenue was in the Amiens house, it was natural that
she should be there too. There were as yet no rules and
constitutions, so that things were in a somewhat fluid

state. Moreover, frequent letters of distress were coming from Bordeaux; repairs must be done to the house, there is no money to pay the workers, the Sisters are making and mending lace that they may be able to live —such were the contents of the letters following each other rapidly from Bordeaux. There was a second house there which needed both a Superior and a Mistress of Novices. Mère Julie was finding this an insoluble problem. "She still had Sœur Jeanne Godelle, who would have been an excellent Superior for Bordeaux," writes Mère Blin, "but she was Mistress of Novices and she served as a corrective to the Novices against the dissipating influence of Mère Victoire." An amazing situation, surely, when a subordinate must be continued in a position as a check to the excesses of a Superior. It is obvious that Mère Victoire had not outgrown "the gush of youth," and this is soon underlined by a few events in Amiens. The letters from Bordeaux had a second urgent appeal in them, for the Sisters there had an ardent desire to have a fixed and definite rule of life, and they urged that Mère Julie should come to them, because Bordeaux was the place where this rule could best be drawn up, since two Fathers of the Faith, men of goodwill and respecters of the primitive spirit, lived there. With all these problems of finance and administration confronting her, it is no wonder if Mère Julie felt bewildered. Indeed, the invitation to Bordeaux was a tempting one, since it offered an immediate solution to the impasse created by the Bishop of Amiens' plan for their rule of life. They could never accept that plan, and the only way out was flight from the diocese. Accordingly, Mère Julie wrote to the Archbishop of Bordeaux, giving him a hint of the situation in Amiens, and begging him to send the Bishop of Amiens a request that she should come to see him.

When his Lordship received this request, he immediately sent for Mère Julie, told her that he could not refuse a wish of the Archbishop of Bordeaux, and fixed her departure for a few days hence. The following day, she received a note from him, cancelling the permission without one word of explanation. This note, in turn, was cancelled, and she finally set off. As she had reason to delay a while in Paris, M. de Sambucy gave her some letters for Monsieur Varin, whom Julie was certain to visit as a friend. Monsieur Varin welcomed her, and then opened the letters she gave him.

"She was thunderstruck by the immediate change in his attitude," writes the chronicler, "for he addressed her with such vigour and vehemence that she became quite faint. He concluded by saying that Monsieur de Sambucy alone should draw up the Rules, that these Rules should be drawn up at Amiens, and that she herself should return there and not leave it. Mère Blin and she were two foolish women, who had stirred up all the Bishops against them. Soon, he predicted, they would not be able to set foot in any diocese, for even the Bishop of Namur had turned against them, etc., etc."

The innocent-looking letters which Mère Julie delivered to her friend consisted solely of a detailed attack on herself and on her actions. It was a trick to hinder the journey to Bordeaux, worthy of him whose methods were like his conversation, as Mère Blin shrewdly observes:

"It is obvious that Monsieur de Sambucy often works towards his ends by many petty means and by deceitful ways of acting; his words are not clear; he throws little remarks into the air which are of a clever subtlety, so that his manner of acting and speaking is so opposed to the utter frankness of Mère Julie, that it was impossible that a bond of sympathy should have existed between them."

It is easy to understand, therefore, how deeply hurt Mère Julie must have been by this strange act of M. de Sambucy.

She left the house of Monsieur Varin, and took her

poor, stricken soul to the feet of her Eucharistic Master. She spent several hours in prayer in the Church of the Visitation, and in the dregs of her chalice she found her consolation. "There was a good priest there," says the record of these years, "who in Confession spoke words of such heavenly grace and healing that she left the church fortified in soul and even in body, resolved to face the return to Amiens, since this was God's Will." She wrote a letter to Mère Blin, saying that she was returning on account of ill-health: this was not the only cause, of course, but it was nevertheless true that the shock to her system from M. de Sambucy's latest piece of intrigue had been so great that it would have been highly imprudent to have continued in Bordeaux. In her memoirs, Mère Blin traces the finger of God in all these happenings. Since the dissolution of the Fathers of the Faith had, according to Monsieur Varin's own wish, broken the bonds of dependence for these Sisters, he had no authority to command a return to Amiens. But God allowed him to do so, in an anger fomented by M. de Sambucy, for the accomplishing of His own almighty designs. For, though Julie had been away but a few days, a state of dramatic tension had developed in the Amiens house.

It all began when, on the return of Mère Blin to Amiens, Mère Victoire, from a sentiment of respect and of gratitude, begged her to take the place of honour in chapel. Mère Blin very prudently declined this, but, as she tells us, "Mère Victoire wept and persevered in begging, so that Mère Julie at last counselled Mère Blin to accept the honour, at least in the refectory." At this juncture, Mère Julie left for Bordeaux. Mère Victoire immediately asked Mère Blin to say the Benedicite before the meal. This request points to the sense of inferiority which she felt in the company of the co-Foundress, though the latter insists that she avoided doing anything that might in the least derogate.

from Mère Victoire's authority. With that power of
analysis which strikes us so often in Mère Blin's notes,
we find the attitude of Mère Victoire shrewdly outlined. "She had indeed sufficient good will, but she
was lacking in simplicity and was carried away by
natural vivacity. And though Mère Julie had made
great efforts to put her at her ease, she was never so,
for indeed she was not in her place." No wonder, therefore, that with such an analytical eye on the situation,
Mère Blin should have had an anxious feeling at the
prospect of being left alone. On the eve of Julie's
departure, she asked her what attitude she should now
adopt. Julie made a complete change in her previous
advice by counselling her to decline all marks of dis-
tinction; however much they might be urged upon her,
with the sole exception of the catechetical instruction,
if this was desired of her, since such function did not
strictly pertain to the duties of Mère Victoire. The
choice of a Sister to teach the Catechism belonged, of
course, to Mère Julie, but the Bishop instructed Monsieur Cottu to give him minute information on all
these matters, and he himself decided so many things
that Mère Julie's authority was becoming more and
more restricted. His attitude towards both the Mothers
was harsh in the extreme, and when he did unbend to
receive them, it was with a glacial "What do you
desire, ladies? " to which was added a peremptory command that there was to be no Mother General, that
Amiens was to be the Mother House, and that Mère
Julie was not to come to him again except by his express
invitation. Some time later, however, Monsieur Cottu
advised them to visit the Bishop. They did so, but
they were met at the door by the valet de chambre who
told them that His Lordship had seen them approach
and declined to receive them. On the heels of this
came a command that Mère Julie should come to him.
Mère Blin, who seems to have had an excellent feeling

for a situation, decided to accompany Mère Julie and to wait for her in a neighbouring house. Her fears were well grounded.

"The precaution of accompanying her," writes Mère Blin, "was not an unnecessary one, for she emerged in tears, and in a state to which none of the other interviews had reduced her. In the depths of her soul there was calm, but the shouting, the harsh tone of voice, the gestures, all combined to bring on an attack of nerves which remained with her for several days. But," continues Mère Blin in a final comment, "Mère Julie's religious sentiments were too profound for the anger of a Bishop to overwhelm them."

Soon after this stormy scene, Mère Julie was authorized to go to Belgium as Namur and Jumet were calling out for her, when an emotional crisis developed at Amiens.

In a hundred ways, Mère Victoire was conscious of her inferiority, and this caused her to suspect and seek out what she considered were deliberate slights to her authority in the most innocent actions. One day there was a titter among some of the young Sisters. Now it is a well-known fact that a titter in the silence of a convent refectory is like a stone dropped in water, a ripple of tittering goes out from it. Unfortunately, however, Mère Victoire had just said a few words in which her lack of education was very apparent. She thought the tittering was for her, and she rose indignantly from the table, left the room, and even left the house. She had gone to pour her troubles in the willing ears of M. de Sambucy and Monsieur Cottu. Mère Blin tells us that she herself "reproved the Sisters, but feebly"—a qualification which clearly hints that she was becoming somewhat tired of the angelic tantrums. Mère Victoire was absent for a considerable time: she returned only to go straight to her room and to bed: at supper, in an atmosphere of tension, everyone said her own Grace in a low voice. It was obvious that Mère

Blin had by this time become thoroughly weary of the state of affairs in Amiens. This was the first opportunity of speaking to the Sisters, and giving them an inkling of the real situation. We give the account as she herself records it in her Memoirs:

"Mère Blin . . . at the end of supper broke the silence to speak to the assembled Sisters as follows: 'You have undoubtedly noticed that something is amiss, and that a storm is muttering around us. We have come together, as you know, to follow the primitive spirit which has been given to us. His Lordship the Bishop does not share our outlook. He will have no Mother General, he is annoyed with our journeying, and there are many other things, of which there would be no point in telling you now, making a cleavage between him and us. We know, Mère Julie and I, who would very willingly receive us if we cannot remain here. We shall go elsewhere, and those who love us will follow.'

"Then," continues Mère Blin, "all the Sisters clapped their hands, and every one without exception cried out—I shall come! . . . I shall come! . . . By these cries, the Sisters eased the tension they felt, and a state of excitement, very restrained however, was in the air."

A few days later, when Mère Julie returned, all was calm again, but it was a calm of fear with all the elements of eruption in it. The whole matter had been considered as criminal and judged as such. Every least lack of formality towards Mère Victoire was now regarded as an act of revolt and disobedience against the Bishop himself. Holy Communion was refused to the Sisters, and they were petrified by constant references to mortal sin and hell fire.

They were severe measures, and Julie respected them for the source from which they came. But she saw clearly that a revolt had been read into a little levity in the young Sisters. It must have been a blow to her, for she had just returned with the abusive words of Monsieur Varin still ringing in her ears.

This rather unfortunate affair brought about one good at least. It set the Bishop, M. de Sambucy, Monsieur Cottu, Monsieur Varin and others who thought as they did, a rather knotty problem, if they attempted to reconcile that unanimous refectory cry— "*c'est moi! . . . c'est moi!*"—with the supposed tiger-ishness and rigidity of Mère Julie Billiart.

CHAPTER NINE

GROPING FOR GOD'S WILL

WHEN one thinks of the history of Notre Dame in the years with which we are now dealing, the image that suggests itself is of a growing stream whose course human hands are trying to shape. But there is an original strength and direction in the water which causes it to bubble through the fingers, run over the hands, escape to the shaping of its own banks. The spirit that breathed on the first spring of Notre Dame would shape the course of its waters, and any other spirit would be a contrary spirit, clouding and eddying its flow. The Amiens house was such an eddy, for contrary spirits were breathing on its waters.

The Rule of a Religious Order is its spirit made flesh. But two spirits cannot animate one body, and therefore the shaping of a Rule of Life for Notre Dame was the coming to grips of these two spirits. There was the spirit of Julie Billiart, a childlike spirit that would incarnate itself in the leading of childlike souls "gently, as a mother does her children," whose charity had no diocesan boundaries to it: there was the spirit of M. de Sambucy, a spirit that would breathe steel into the soft lines of this incarnation, so as to shape Notre Dame according to a pattern of ancient monasticism, or rather, of ancient monasticism according to the pattern and parochial mind of M. de Sambucy.

In whatever way she may have conceived and expressed it, Julie Billiart was clearly conscious of all the

implications of those angry words which Monsieur
Varin addressed to her when she stood trembling
before him under the lash of M. de Sambucy's accusations. "Monsieur de Sambucy alone shall draw up the
Rule." She had her orders to beg Monsieur l'Abbé de
Sambucy to draw up the Rule, and in this command she
saw the Will of God. Accordingly, she lost no time in
getting to Monsieur l'Abbé, and "she spoke several
times with him," notes the ever-watchful Mère Blin,
"without resentment and even in too open and trusting
a manner." Monsieur l'Abbé received the proposition
with great pleasure, vaguely arranged many talks on
details with the two Mothers, which materialized in
but three or four conversations, where everything
that was said served only to underline the complete divergence of view. Nothing final was put on
paper.

In the midst of all this, a letter which had been long
overdue arrived for Mère Blin from the Bishop of
Namur. He was resigned to the delay in her return,
but only just resigned, and says he is happy in the
thought that the hearty welcome she knows awaits her
and the sighs of her daughters must surely hasten her
return. The letter finishes with solicitous enquiries
about her health, and warm greetings to her and to
Mère Julie—"with which," he concludes, "I leave you
at the feet of Christ, pierced as was His Heart for us."
Mère Julie and Mère Blin replied to this letter, letting
the Bishop know that Amiens had become a centre of
storms, and that it looked as though he might be asked
to shelter not Mère Blin only, but the whole community of Notre Dame. The Bishop's reply was a
cordial one.

"Your worthy Bishop will give good reason for all this to
your Mother General, at least I hope he will. As to my diocese,
we shall think ourselves happy in having you, you and Mère

Julie and all the companions you will bring. I wish only that we had a bigger residence, but God, to Whose Will we must conform in all things, will find one for us, if so it pleases Him."

Things were twisting themselves into a Gordian knot at Amiens, and this letter seemed indeed a sword poised above the knot, ready to cut to a clean solution at a "fiat" from the Foundress. But though her lips trembled on that "fiat," she could not bring herself to say it, for fear of running counter to God's Will made her reluctant to act on anything less than a clear command from the Bishop of Amiens to leave the diocese. She contented herself with showing the letter to Monsieur l'Abbé de Sambucy, that he might know they would not remain in Amiens merely because they had nowhere else to go. She hoped that this would help to bring matters to a head and to a solution, for things were impossible and it was becoming more and more difficult to do the least action in accordance with the primitive spirit. Yet Julie suffered all this in silence, while she waited, with tremendous patience, with quiet, unwavering confidence, for a sign from God. "She often said to me," writes Mère Blin, "that God would settle everything, that we would be amazed how clear everything would become, so that we would see our way open before us." These were not mere words said to comfort an anxious companion, but they welled up warm from the springs of confidence in the heart of a woman who had the simplicity and the divine directness of a child.

"She will never learn," we often say of a person who persists in showing the simplicity of the dove where we consider the wisdom of the serpent would pay greater dividends. It is a comment like this that we are inclined to jot in the margin of the early accounts of Mère Julie's conversations with Monsieur l'Abbé de Sambucy at this time. Artlessly she speaks of the rigid requirements of the Bishop of Amiens, and by contrast, of the little demanded by the Bishop of Namur, who merely asks to see their annual register.   How wisely would we have kept silence on these things, knowing what would happen, we think in our wisdom; indeed, with what straight and clear lines would we not design the whole fabric of life, and yet God continues to use crooked lines to write straight!   And the paradox is this: only with the straight, simple, large lines of a mind like that of Julie Billiart can God make his glorious design of crooked lines.   So it were as well for us to put away the sharp-pointed pencil and the deadly accurate straight edge we so often reach wisely towards Him. . . . Of course, Monsieur l'Abbé de Sambucy did precisely as we would have expected him to do, remembering what Julie seems to have forgotten, the letters which made of her her own executioner.   Monsieur l'Abbé seems to have been a man who knew how to reserve his fire and how to choose his moment.   He chose it now.

Facts, figures, coldly reasoned accusations crowded the letter that came one day to the Bishop of Namur from Monsieur l'Abbé de Sambucy.   Julie's remark on how little the Bishop demanded became a triumphant and unanswerable proof of her burning desire for independence, and round it were heaped words and phrases quoted to M. de Sambucy in openness and confidence from the Bishop's letters to Julie: words and phrases which he possibly intended for herself alone. Served back in this way, Monsieur l'Abbé knew that they were calculated to create an impression of a certain craftiness with even a dash of duplicity in it.   This impression was indeed made, but only for a very short time, for duplicity and the mind of Julie Billiart were as darkness and light.

Meantime, the deadlock over the composing of a Rule of Life continued.   M. Cottu now undertook to draw up the Rules and informed the Mothers that he was working on them. They received the news with a sort of calm resignation to the inevitable, for they knew that the mind of M. Cottu in all that concerned Notre Dame was merely a clear-glass window on the mind of M. de Sambucy. Other worries crowded themselves on Mère Julie and Mère Blin, for a letter arrived from Namur to remind them of the tangled state of things there and to urge them to send a Sister as soon as possible to act as Superior in place of Sœur Xavier, who was now a permanent invalid. Mère Julie gave this and other matters requiring attention in Jumet and elsewhere as reasons for requesting leave to make another journey. Though it was the policy of the authorities at Amiens to ignore her title of Mother General, Monsieur Cottu could not refuse her request, since it concerned matters outside the diocese. She accordingly set off once again, leaving Mère Blin to look after matters in Amiens, not, however, without giving her some advice and counsel. Mère Blin must have shared the feelings of a ship's look-out who finds himself approaching rocks and shallows on which his vessel has hitherto almost foundered. But an unexpected development was to ensure a measure of internal tranquillity. Something else ensured it, too. Fever swept through the Amiens community, and in the rush of attending the sick there was no time for brooding on slights to personal dignity.

Perhaps one of the traits which Julie Billiart's biographers have too lightly stressed, is her fine, practical psychology, or as she herself might have put it simply, her shrewd peasant wisdom, redolent of the clean soil and rich crops of Picardy. Her judgments on people were expressed in rather misleadingly simple terms: only in the light of later events does one really see how effectively they went to the heart of the matter and summed up everything else. Her simple judgment on Sœur Victoire—she needs action—comes really alive in Mère Blin's account of this fever in the Amiens house. We see Sœur Victoire in a new light: for a brief space of time she is the fine character she might have been if she had not been clumsily moulded contrary to the wise design of her Mother, by well-meaning, bad psychologists who failed to realize that they were dealing with the stuff of a Martha rather than that of a Mary.

"Fever invaded the house at this time," writes Mère Blin, "and nearly all the Sisters were attacked by it. Four Sisters were sick for two or three months, so severely indeed that, during long periods they seemed to have almost lost their reason. Mère Victoire, whose energetic health had a tireless charity in it, was almost continually by the bedside of the sick."

Gone is the Mère Victoire created and named by M. de Sambucy, promoted for imaginary qualities of leadership, conscious of her incompetence and with all the touchiness that goes with such a situation: a Martha made to play the rôle of a contemplative, finding an outlet for her suppressed energy in ascetic exaggerations which could have brought ruin to the movement she was supposed to inspire. However, others were touchy for her, so that the cry of slighted authority is not missing even here. Exhausted from her constant attendance on the sick, Mère Victoire did not consider herself equal to the task of preparing the Catechism lesson for the Sisters. She therefore deputed Mère Blin to do so. As soon, however, as news of this reached the Bishop, he sent word "that when Mère Victoire was unable to give the instruction, no one else was to give it." It is a pity that this hint of unpleasantness and suspicion should shadow a page, beautiful with the beauty of Sisters thinking and working in harmony. It served to emphasize what is already abundantly clear:

that the tangle in these first years of Notre Dame was due to strange fingers touching the loom.

Following in the footsteps of Julie on her journey to Namur, we are reminded of that passage in St. Paul where, after enumerating many trials, he goes on to say: "Besides those things which are of my daily instance, the solicitude for all the Churches." Only in occasional stray phrases of the Epistles do we get a hint of just what that last phrase, which seems but a cadence at the end of a sentence, meant for St. Paul: "the solicitude for all the Churches." In the memoirs of Julie Billiart, we find constant evidence of what her solicitude for all her houses really entailed. In every house, at every stage of her career, she met with personal problems of individual Sisters. Two of these will serve as typical both of the problems and of her approach to them.

Sœur Xavier, who ruled the Namur community from a sick-bed, was the problem of zeal not sufficiently tempered by tact and prudence. Mère Blin has etched her character very neatly:

"Though well mellowed by her own personal spiritual progress, she lacked the mellowing of experience, was over-eager for the advancement of her Sisters and spoke to them with that extra emphasis of authority which prevented her from gaining their confidence. The Sisters were afraid to open their hearts to her, and an atmosphere of constraint, not conducive to progress in virtue, was the result. Mère Julie saw clearly that things could not continue long on that footing, but the remedy was not nearly so clear. As in all such cases, she abandoned everything into the hands of Jesus and Mary, confident that she would be shown, both as to time and to place, what she must do."

We like to linger for a moment on words like these. Julie Billiart could lead her children "gently, as a mother," because she herself had the heart of a child. In all their problems, her children stretched out their

hands to her, and in the clasp of her hand they felt
Christ. If she saw no immediate solution to their problem, her own hand went gropingly to God, not in
agitated fear, not in the anxiety which provoked the
rebuke of Christ on His Disciples, but with the calm-
ness, the simple confidence with which a child seeks
for the hand of its mother.

Sœur Geneviève Gosselin presented a problem of quite
a different kind, for when Mère Julie visited the St.-
Nicolas house, she found Sœur Saint Jean and Sœur
Catherine very troubled indeed. Occasionally in con-
vents a type of nun is met with, restless, unsettling to
herself and to her companions, and obsessed with the
idea that she would be happy if only she were allowed
to do a certain type of work, usually of a kind for which
she is obviously unfit. Such, it would seem, was Sœur
Geneviève.

" While in the Amiens house, she had been obedient to Mère
Julie," writes Mère Blin, " but being of a narrow and stubborn
disposition, she apparently did not understand that she was
bound to show equal obedience to other superiors. Sœur Saint
Jean and Sœur Catherine had complained of this on several
occasions, and Mère Julie had threatened to send her away.
This Sister was obsessed by a too natural attraction for the
boarders. She was content only when with them, everything
else was repugnant to her, and she determined to avoid anything that could prevent her following her inclination. Mère
Julie spoke to her in words that had a deep and overflowing
charity in them . . . and Sœur Geneviève was changed and
converted, but only for a time."

The outcome of all this was inevitable. Sœur
Geneviève left the convent. It was no small grief, in
the midst of a multitude of griefs, that the third Sister
who enlisted under her banner should have grown
weary and turned back.

On her return to Amiens, Mère Julie found some of
the Sisters still sick with fever.

" Two of these," writes Mère Blin, "after a few months illness, had almost lost their reason. As one of them absolutely insisted on going home, Mère Julie accompanied her on a twelve-league journey, which was both exhausting and filled with many incidents. The other Sister was persuaded to return to her own home for convalescence, and as she lived in the town, her mother came to accompany her."

Three others, about the solidity of whose vocation there were grave doubts, among them being a trouble-maker between the Bishop and the Sisters to whom Mère Blin constantly and somewhat caustically refers as "la Parisienne," left the convent. This sickness, as the chronicler remarks, was the fan with which the floor of Notre Dame was purged. Only the strong and the faithful remained in the Amiens house to stand firm in the great upheaval now close at hand.

One morning, a little later, Monsieur Cottu handed Mère Julie a sheaf of papers. "Here," he said in effect, "is your complete Rule of Life, based on that of the ancient Sœurs de Notre Dame de Bordeaux, which, in its turn, was drawn from that of the Jesuits." It seemed, indeed, a noble lineage. But when the Mothers looked over it together, they found that it was, as Mère Blin put it, "an edifice without a foundation." There was no point in discussing the design of the superstructure. No Mother General, no visitation, no houses outside the one diocese of Amiens ("although," says Mère Blin in a parenthesis, "we had already some houses in other dioceses, before coming under the special authority of the Bishop of Amiens"), the strictures were already too familiar to the Foundresses. They did not think it advisable to speak their mind openly once again at this stage, so they parried for time: there were certain amendments that might perhaps be made, the time was not quite ripe for the establishing of a full rule, perhaps Monsieur Cottu would leave things in abeyance for a year or so and study the trend of events. But it was all to no purpose. Monsieur Cottu very soon pressed for an explanation of their reluctance to accept the Rule he had drawn up. Then they spoke their minds clearly. Followed an angry and peremptory order from the Bishop that they should accept the Rule and pronounce their vows in accordance with it on the Feast of the Annunciation. It was time, he added, that good order was established in the house. "On this," says Mère Blin, "we held our peace." The stage was set for the last act of the Amiens drama in the history of Notre Dame. The development of that act was determined by two things: a quiet, respectful resolution, on the one hand, and a deep, calm confidence born of simplicity and of prayer on the other. The first accelerated the course of events: the second fixed the mood.

The resolution was taken by Mère Blin, as financial head of Notre Dame. In her Memoirs, she records her words to Monsieur Cottu: "Father, since everything seems to be going from bad to worse and there does not seem to be any solution, I assure you that I shall take the Mother and her flock to Namur." This, we are told, together with the answer Mère Julie gave to the Bishop when he demanded to know why Mère Blin should depart some morning, taking all her possessions with her.

This state of affairs which, in Mère Blin's vivid phrase, was one of "thorns and darkness," was nevertheless bathed in the calm confidence of the intense prayer of Julie Billiart. She prayed long and deeply, and her prayers were as child-hands reaching towards God through the darkness, groping among the thorns. Against such prayer, God has pronounced Himself helpless: therefore, on the fifth day of her prayer, she spoke to her children in words that had the great heart of her simplicity in them: "I am not now shadowed with the least unrest; I feel within me a profound calm. The Holy Infant Jesus has taken us under His protec-

tion. He will deliver us. . . ." These words from
their Mother were as manna in the desert. In their
strength her followers found strength, to stand firm
and be found faithful when the storm and the darkness
should have passed, and the thorns should prove to
have been but the testing time in the growth of the
rose. . . .

Two days later Monsieur Cottu was shown into Mère
Julie's room. He had come from Monseigneur, he said,
"to speak his mind," and, judging by Mère Blin's
account, he does not seem to have minced words in
doing so. Finally he threatened that the Bishop "would
wash his hands of our affairs, withdraw our Chaplain
and refuse to establish any Rule, if Mère Blin refused
to give a preliminary assurance that her possessions
would be devoted to the Amiens house." To this whirlwind of words, Mère Julie replied calmly and simply:
"Father, these are matters which do not depend on any
decision of mine. I shall go and seek Mère Blin."
There are times when a sudden detail in a chronicle
makes it intimately alive, as though the narrator had
begun to act the narrative. Such a moment, in Mère
Blin's Chronicle, is her account of how she was summoned to the room. "Then Mère Julie went to Mère
Blin's room, which adjoined her own. Not being able
to give any better indication, she pointed up above her
head to suggest that affairs had risen to a critical pitch,
while she said aloud: 'Come and speak with Monsieur
Cottu.'" It was in a much calmer tone that Monsieur
Cottu repeated the proposition to Mère Blin, for it
was much easier to be high-handed and angry with the
humble Julie than with her companion, who could,
when it served a good purpose, be again the haughty
aristocrat who had brought the clamouring "Agents de
la Nation" to an uncomfortable silence with a level
look and a calm question. There is little reason to suppose that, as a Sister of Notre Dame, she actually did

this: but there is evidence that she could sometimes suggest such reserves by a certain shading of tone in a perfectly respectful sentence. One suspects that Monsieur Cottu caught something of that shading as he listened to Mère Blin's answer: that this was not a matter for a moment's decision, that they must be given time to consider, that the advice of prudent and enlightened persons must be sought. Is it fanciful to notice certain overtones in that "prudent and enlightened" which may well have left Monsieur Cottu feeling much less at his ease?

"Prudent and enlightened" advice came in plenty. Monsieur Duminy, Curé of the Cathedral, spoke his mind. Monsieur Chevalier, Curé of Rubempré, spoke his mind. Both assured them that they were under no obligation to accept Rules that were foreign to their primitive spirit. But they hesitated, still groping for the certain Will of God.

Meanwhile, matters were going from bad to worse with the Notre Dame community at Namur. They had taken over a new house, the number of boarders had greatly increased, and problems arose which were beyond the capacity and the experience of the Sisters. Sœur Xavier, their Superior, was rapidly approaching her end: the Sister who acted as cook was rendered helpless and a nervous wreck by temptations which shattered her peace of soul, and spread unrest among her companions. Letter after letter was dispatched to Mère Julie: letters in which many things were suppressed because of the anxieties they knew to be heaped up already for their beloved Mother, but which that motherly heart sensed behind the reticence. Mère Blin has given a pathetic picture of the distress of these poor Sisters, for whom everything was getting more impossible and unaccountable every day. One gathers that they had come together for a meal, only to find that because of the helplessness of the cook there was

either nothing, or that little which is worse than nothing, to eat. There had been a great sense of indirection about everything in the house because of their
Superior's illness, now rapidly taking a fatal turn: the
boarders were a constant source of problems: there had
as yet been no word from their beloved Mère Julie
with the longed-for "I am coming": nerves were
frayed, and now this little vexation, as so often happens
with people who have borne great strain, seemed the
culminating point of misery. "They were so dis-
heartened on sitting down to table," writes Mère Blin,
"that they burst into tears."

Meantime Mère Julie was pressing for permission to
leave for Namur, but the Bishop was insistent that she
should not. He would be very pleased, he said, to allow
Mère Blin to return there, but Mère Julie saw plainly
the danger of this, in the present disturbed state of
affairs in Amiens. As before, advisers were at hand, telling her that she had every reason to disobey, but she
hesitated and went into conference with Mère Blin
and Mère Victoire.

"It was an astonishing thing," comments Mère Blin, "to see
Mère Victoire called to this most intimate council: but Mère
Julie concealed scarcely anything from her, and was in the habit
of dealing with her with great openness of heart, on many
occasions giving her proof of the confidence she placed in her.
Mère Victoire loved and reverenced her, but she was young,
volatile, a victim to sentiments which she scarcely understood,
and wholly under the thumb of Monsieur de Sambucy."

Advice and a plan came from Monsieur Cottu, but
Mère Julie would not act on them, for, says Mère Blin,
"she was in one of those moments of uncertainty, when
one goes forward inch by cautious inch, groping one's
way."

They were days of awful anxiety. The Sisters who
surrounded Mère Julie were lacking in acquired

talents, and though full of goodwill, were also rich in imperfections on account of the muddled and myopic policy that had created a state of spiritual morass among them.   Everything had combined to produce that troubled state beloved of hell, and every Sister in those last days of the Amiens house had her own desert of aridity and her own demon to torment her.

"In the retreat given by Monsieur Cottu," writes Mère Blin, "they were, in spite of all their efforts, troubled, dissipated, exhausted, tormented, each in her own way, with a host of temptations, and there was nothing to greet them when they came out of retreat, save a yet more muddled and frustrating state of affairs."

There is a strange medley here of conflicting aims, of uncertainty, of groping, of exhaustion from fruitless waiting, of temptation, of frustration, that could not have gone on much longer.   There is, therefore, an almost audible sigh of relief accompanying the sentence in which Mère Blin finishes this section of her Memoirs: "Finally, the moment of unravelling came on the morning of January the twelfth."   This sentence strikes a chord of harmony like a phrase of music lifting itself clearly out of a welter of dissonance, a phrase that will rise and dominate, however much the dissonance may again threaten to drown it.   For the great trial which Julie Billiart had mysteriously known in those now far-off Compiègne days was at the beginning of its end.

On January 12th, then, Monsieur Cottu came to Mère Julie's room again and handed her a letter, dictated by the Bishop, but written and signed by Monsieur Cottu, his Vicar General.

"Mère Blin and Mère Julie were occupying the house," the letter stated, "on the understanding that they were to form an establishment of Sisters of Notre Dame, but, since Mère Julie was clearly leading her daughters in an entirely different spirit, she could retire to any diocese she wished, for, as far as the

Bishop was concerned, he intended to take over the house and form and fashion therein real Sisters of Notre Dame."

With what relief must Mère Julie have read that letter! Not, indeed, that she wished to escape from a trying and heartrending situation, for she was no coward, but her relief was the relief experienced at the end of a long, groping search.

She had moved forward, inch by inch, fearful only of doing her own will, seeking calmly, groping prayerfully, holding aloft the white lamp of her single-minded simplicity. Its white light shimmered always on a wedding-garment that was unspotted by the events and the motives that crossed and re-crossed perplexingly in the mist. It was a long way, a way of pain, but the lamp had not been opaque from breath of self and its light had not been dimmed. . . .

Then, suddenly, the Will for which she sought was clear to her: a Hand clasped hers, the Hand for which she had long and patiently groped. She felt its luminous shadow on her like a caress, and she knew the blessing that came with it.

But had that Hand held instead of the order to go forward with her life-work the strangely loving decree that she was to be flung down again in helplessness, her work crumbled and forgotten, she would still have lifted it and its sentence and pressed them to her lips.

For His Will was her peace.

CHAPTER TEN

WALKING THROUGH COBWEBS

MÈRE Julie stood with the letter she had just read in her hand. At the door, Monsieur Cottu paused, hesitated a few seconds, and then asked:

"Whom do you propose to take with you straight away?"

"Why," Julie answered thoughtfully, "I shall take this Sister and that Sister," naming different members of the Amiens house. Among them she mentioned Sœur Ciska Steenhaut, a young Flemish girl of Ghent, aged seventeen, with an excellent knowledge of French, who had attracted the attention and interest of M. de Sambucy to such an extent that he was determined to keep her in Amiens.

The Chronicler records this exchange of conversation:

"Don't mention her," said Monsieur Cottu, "let her remain."

"But, mon Père," she answered, "have you not just now said that I must take them all?"

"Well, I am telling you now to leave her," he said. "It is not certain that his Lordship does not wish to retain a few of the Sisters."

"Mon Père," she went on, "of one thing I am perfectly certain, and that is that she will not wish to remain."

"All the same, let her remain," he said.

"I assure you," she repeated, "that she will not wish it."

"Why must you persist in dogged opposition," he said impatiently. "It is your constant opposition that makes you so displeasing to the Bishop. . . ."

Seeing the anger mounting in Monsieur Cottu, Mère Blin, with a quick preliminary look at Mère Julie, broke in:

"Mon Père," she said, "out of consideration for you, she shall remain."

"Yes," added Mère Julie, "I shall leave her free to remain. Mon Père, I promise you that they will all be left perfectly free in this matter."

"Very good," said Monsieur Cottu, "leave them all free, use no persuasion."

The persuasion was to come from Monsieur Cottu himself. He had scarcely left the house when a message arrived summoning Sœur Ciska to him. She had a suspicion of what was afoot, and she went anxiously to her Mother.

"It is for you to choose, my child," she said quietly. "You are perfectly free. Think over it well."

"But, my Mother," she protested earnestly, "I have already done my thinking. Nothing can change me, for I belong to you for life, and nothing can alter that."

"Go, my child," Mère Julie said, "I am confident that God will be with you. Speak little."

It is pleasing to linger over this conversation, recorded for us in the annals. There is a beauty in it of the mother-daughter relationship that always existed between Julie and her Sisters. There is the lovely devotion of a girl of seventeen. And finally, there are those two words of immense common sense at the end, enshrining a wisdom which Mère Julie had learned from sad experience in dealing with these ecclesiastical superiors. Ciska listened to them well.

Monsieur Cottu received her graciously, making her sit down.

"Doubtless," he began, in a tone of flattering deference, "you have heard that Mère Julie is about to depart. What do you think of that?"

"Mon Père," she answered quietly, "I shall go with her."

"But, my child," he urged, "you will lose your soul, for you are taking the wrong road. Mère Julie is the victim of her own illusions."

"I belong to my Mother," she answered, "and I shall follow her."

"You know I shall refuse to give you Holy Communion, if you disobey. His Lordship does not wish you to depart."

"I shall follow my Mother," she calmly persisted.

"In the end," writes Mère Blin, "when he had exhausted all his eloquence in a vain attempt to shake her resolution, he took her to the apartments of Monsieur de Sambucy, who lived with him, and left her there alone while Leonard went out to seek Monsieur. When he returned, Monsieur de Sambucy had a few words with Monsieur Cottu as to the state of affairs, and then he entered the room abruptly. He began immediately to hurl the judgments of God upon Ciska, warning her that she would be a prey to terror and desolation on her death-bed if she disobeyed. That if she followed her Mother to Namur, Mgr. Pisani would get his friend the Bishop of Ghent to pack her off back to Amiens. To all this she replied that she had always been attached to Mère Julie and Mère Blin, and that she did not wish to be separated from them. 'That is merely the voice of nature,' he urged. 'You ought to obey, for Mère Julie is the victim of illusions, and it is I who have grace for your soul, it is I who am gifted with light to lead you. You have always had confidence in me and I have always had confidence in you. If this were in Confession, I would have something quite different to say to you." He repeated these last words several times, but she did not take the implied invitation. The only

answer he could get from her was that she was her
Mother's daughter, and that she would follow her any-
where. 'Well, stay for four days,' he added, 'and then
you may follow her.' 'No,' she answered, 'if I remain,
I shall be given someone else for my Mother.'"

At this point Monsieur Cottu entered, said a few
word in Latin to M. de Sambucy and took Ciska away
to the Bishop. On the way, he stopped deliberately
and impressively several times, and spoke to her with
great vehemence, calculated either to persuade or to
intimidate her. They did neither. When she was
shown in to the Bishop, she knelt, asked and received
his blessing. He then motioned her, with a smile, to
a chair. This time a more diplomatic approach was to
be attempted.

"Sœur Ciska," began Monsieur Cottu, "has some
doubts about following her Mother."

The young nun muttered that she had no doubts
about the matter, and when they asked what she wished
to do, she answered :

"I belong to my Mother and I shall not leave her."

"You are an ignorant girl," the Bishop said, all
affability gone, "and you don't know your Catechism."

He went on to quote the commandment which en-
joins obedience to spiritual Pastors. When he had
enlarged on this for a while, Monsieur Cottu said to
her :

"You will be sent to a boarding-school where you
can instruct children."

"Mon Père," she answered, "I know nothing, so of
what use could I be? "

"That is quite enough," His Lordship cut in angrily.
She rose, knelt before him and asked his blessing.
Instead, she received a shower of mortifying words.

"That same day," notes the Chronicler, "Mère Julie
received a letter from Monsieur de Sambucy, in which
he tried to persuade her that if she took Sœur Ciska

with her she would offend the Bishop of Namur, who
would be himself placed in an embarrassing position
and would therefore command that she be sent back.
Monsieur de Sambucy, relying on his long-standing
friendship with the Bishop of Ghent, thought that he
could influence this affair as he wished, but it was not
so.   That Bishop had opened his eyes to the evidence
of facts, and the inconsistency in Monsieur de Sambucy's conduct was only too obvious."

The efforts to win over this young nun are as amazing as they are puerile.   On analysis, they hardly seem
more than an attempt to retain something from the
defeat, as a sop to wounded pride.   It is part of those
last unsettling days in Amiens, and it serves but as a
final, and unfortunately very heavy, underlining to the
pettiness which inspired the entire opposition.   M. de
Sambucy felt the first shock of his undermined credit,
in his failure to sway the Bishop of Namur.   He was
further shattered by a letter from his Superior, Père
Varin, who had also come alive to the web of pettiness
of which he had been made an unconscious and an un-
willing part.   "Even if the whole world was against
Mère Julie," it read, "you, you at least, should have
undertaken her defence."   This, to the head and front
of the attack on her!   Moreover, his letter to the Bishop
of Ghent had come to Père Varin's notice, and he was
far from pleased.   "The intention may have been all
right, but the consequences were far from being so."
If there is one thing the bravest of men flinch from, it
is the thought of having made a fool of themselves.   And
M. de Sambucy knew that he had done so.   There are
times, too, when a straight rebuke reveals the fact that
we have been wilfully blinding ourselves.   It was so for
M. de Sambucy, for temporarily, at any rate, he showed
repentance.   He took up his pen to make reparation for
the real wrong he had done to Julie Billiart.   He sent
letters to the Vicar General of the Bishop of Bordeaux,

to the Bishops of Ghent and Tournai, whose minds he had assiduously seeded with misrepresentation against her. The influence of M. de Sambucy in high places was on the wane.

The eventful day of January 12th, 1809, was drawing to a close, and an air of expectancy filled the room in which the Sisters were having their evening meal. It was broken by Mère Julie rising and speaking to them in a quiet, rather tired voice, for the day had been one of great strain. She outlined the situation for them clearly and concisely. Because they would not accept propositions which were contrary to their primitive spirit, both she and Mère Blin had been expelled from Amiens by the Bishop. In a silence stiff with tension, she concluded in the same quiet tone: "Those among you who love us, will follow us. But you are all perfectly free to choose." In the unanimous chorus of ayes that greeted her words, no avowal was more vehement than that of Mère Victoire. "If I remain," she cried out, "it will be because I have been cast into prison. I shall follow my Mother." One is irresistibly reminded of Peter's vehement confidence, by Mère Blin's account of the sequel: "She continued in these sentiments for some weeks, but continued attacks on her resolution, together with her great confidence in the judgment of Monsieur de Sambucy, combined with her own weakness and volatility to vanquish her."

The next two days were very busy ones for Julie, but she was one of those people who have the rare gift of getting things done thoroughly, quickly, quietly, without surrounding themselves and everyone and everything with a fog of fuss. Anything worth sending so far was despatched in advance, and Mère Blin was given instructions as to the disposal of the rest. It was likely that some of the Sisters would not remain firm, so precise instructions were given as to how they were to be regarded and treated. It was a matter of wonder to the good Madame de Franssu, ardent admirer of Julie, how she did so many things together, and yet kept everything in the tranquillity of order.

But the opposition was not quite finished yet. On the morning of the second day, Monsieur Cottu came into Mère Julie's room, where she, Mère Blin and Sœur Ciska were busily tying parcels. He looked on for a moment and then said: "Sœur Ciska, are you still bent on going?" "Yes, mon Père," and went on quietly tying her knots. Monsieur Cottu had previously announced that the Bishop intended to retain Sœurs Victoire, Ciska and Clotilde. Mère Julie had answered that they were all free to choose, but the determination of Sœur Ciska to follow her was so strong that it pointed to a great vocation to Notre Dame, and therefore Julie was equally determined that Ciska should not be forced. Ciska had hardly spoken when the door opened again to admit M. de Sambucy.

"He had in his pocket," writes Mère Blin, "a letter from the Bishop which, though it was intended for Mère Julie, was neither addressed nor sealed. With an embarrassed air he drew it from his pocket, but it was so vehement a letter that he hesitated to put it into Mère Julie's hands. He finally compromised by reading it and then putting it again into his pocket. Monseigneur's style surpassed itself. The gist of it was that he wished the house to be left just as it was, that the chapel should remain untouched also, and that the three Sisters he had named should remain. Mère Julie quietly replied that all the furnishings of both houses and chapel had been bought with Mère Blin's money, were needed for the Namur house, and did not belong in any way to the Bishop."

There was still a spark of the old anger in M. de Sambucy, and it showed now. Turning to Julie, he said:

"You will make yourself Mother General at any cost!"

"Mon Père," came the quiet reply, "let the Bishop

appoint me to tend the fowl, and he will see by my submission whether I covet the name or honour of Mother General."

She was struggling to have that title recognized for Notre Dame, but her struggle was not for personal honour. Mother General meant freedom to make necessary journeys, and the necessary authority to preserve and maintain, in union with the Bishops, good order in all her establishments.

Events like these filled the three days between the delivery of the letters and Mère Julie's departure. One of her biographers has given this simple and moving account of the final scene:

"One o'clock had just chimed from the tower of the beautiful cathedral when, for the last time, Mère Julie stood in the midst of the assembled community in that city of Amiens where she had suffered so many tribulations, received so many graces. In a voice broken by tears she bade them farewell, and then, while all her daughters wept around her, she and her five companions got into the cart which was to be their travelling equipage, and took the high road to Belgium."

It was bitterly cold, and the wheels of the carriage crunched on the icy road. The Sisters felt that the air they breathed was like ice entering their lungs, driving the heat from every part of their bodies. Before long, the road rose in a steep incline and the horses began to stumble. Their conductor, a raw, uncouth fellow, gruffly ordered them out to walk alongside, which they were obliged to do for five or six hours. The sky was heavy, snow was stinging their faces, and icy needles seemed to be penetrating every part of their bodies. But the joy and courage of their Mothers, stepping out bravely before them, sustained their spirits, and so they reached their first stopping-place.

Even in daylight the inn at which they halted would have seemed sinister, but with the shades of night

THIS IS NOT THE PLACE FOR YOU

gathering about it, it looked positively evil: "More like a cave than an inn," Mère Blin noted. When they entered, a number of criminal-looking faces turned to survey them from the card-table, with a glance that was half curious and half hostile and by no means pleasant to see. Almost immediately these men rose and left the inn, saying they would be back presently. It flashed upon Julie that they had fallen into a den of thieves. Not to awaken suspicion, however, she accepted the frugal supper which was set before them in plates of very questionable cleanliness, and then she went a little way along the high road to explore the surroundings. As she walked on, lifting her heart to God in earnest prayer, she suddenly saw before her a youth of dignified and modest bearing, who accosted her with these words: "This is not the place for you! Go further on. Fly from this house." She wished to question her kind friend, but he had disappeared.

She was retracing her steps, full of what had occurred, when two of her Sisters ran to meet her saying, "Ma Mère, we have just seen a kind and venerable old woman who said to us, 'Sisters, this is not the place for you, go further on. Fly from this house.' We wanted to bring her to you, but she had disappeared."

Evidently this was a warning from heaven; but how were they to get away? It was late, the horses had been taken out, the luggage removed from the coach, the rooms and beds prepared. No matter: they must leave there and then. Mère Julie went to rouse the driver, and by means of kind words and a tip, persuaded him to push on farther. She then asked to see the bed-rooms, and when the host pointed to the two wretched couches in the single apartment of which the would-be inn consisted, telling her that he and his family would pass the night in the loft, she said that she could not consent to such an arrangement, and would seek another lodging.

"At the same instant," to use her own words, "and without our being able to explain it otherwise than by the intervention of the Angels, my daughters and all their packages were some- how or other in their places on the coach, the horses put to and waiting the signal to start. We pursued our way rapidly in spite of loud opposition from the innkeeper, and in a short time we reached a village where we were able to pass the night without mishap. When I considered all the circumstances of this event, and above all the very rapid manner in which we had got off from the inn, I could not help seeing in it the Hand of Divine Providence, who by means of His Angels had delivered us from a great danger."

When the people of the neighbouring village learnt what had happened, they congratulated the Sisters on having escaped from a regular nest of brigands, and a house of such ill repute that for some time past the eyes of the police had been upon it.

Meantime there were moments of drama at Amiens. Monsieur Fournier, Vicar General of Amiens, accom- panied by the Superior of the Seminary, came to the house at a moment when Mère Victoire had mounted a carriage, due to leave next day with Sœur Godelle and her companions, in order to arrange their luggage.

"Are you leaving too?" Monsieur Fournier asked.

"Not this time," she answered.

He continued his way to the refectory and sent for Mère Blin. No sooner had she entered the room than, dispensing with all preliminaries, he launched an attack on Mère Julie: she was a rebel, in opposition to the Gospel where Christ said to His Apostles: "He that heareth you, heareth Me; he that despiseth you, des- piseth Me."

On all this Mère Blin makes one of the most delight- fully devastating comments in her whole Chronicle: "He continued to utter many sentiments at once beautiful and good, lacking only a truer application of their meaning, and a calmer tone in their expression." The nerves of his face were contracted, she notes, revealing that he was suffering violence, "for doubtless the enemy of man was throwing his soul into confusion." Having prefaced his remarks with the thunders of the Gospel, he went on:

"The Bishop of Amiens has sent a letter to Namur justifying his course of action, and do not delude yourself that the Bishop of Namur will receive the Sisters with graciousness, for the Bishops support each other."

"We shall know that very soon," she replied, "for I am expecting a letter any day now."

"The Bishop," he said, returning to his former line of argument, "has every reason to be incensed against Mère Julie. Her hard, imperious nature has placed a yoke of iron on her daughters."

"If so, Monsieur," she continued, "why do they all wish to follow her?"

"The human spirit can lead a strange dance," he answered. "Her disobedience——"

"But, Monsieur, in what has she been disobedient?"

"Why," he exclaimed, "by opposing the good order which the Bishop strove to establish in the house."

"Monsieur," she said levelly, "I regard it as a decision of providence that she should leave this house."

"Yes, yes," he answered impatiently, "a decision of her own pig-headedness."

"The Bishop has treated her with great harshness."

"And with great goodness, too," he answered, "when she returned from Paris to cast herself at his feet. All this has caused great affliction to his Lordship. From motives of pride she did not come to ask his blessing before she departed."

"I am very sorry that his Lordship has been troubled," she answered, "for, if God blesses us, our Sisters will be ever at his service."

"Oh, be assured of one thing," he went on, "that he will never have any need of you. The Bishop is coming here this morning to assemble the Sisters and bid them choose between their Bishop and Mère Julie. And his Lordship," he added with a little lift of triumph in his voice, "has great piety, great knowledge and a most persuasive eloquence. The authority and presence of the Bishop will have an immediate effect."

Then, turning to the priest who accompanied him, he began to sing the praises of the Bishop of Namur. A man of intellect and of shrewdness, a man who listens to both clocks striking, who examines both sides of a question one after the other. . . . This was meant as a master-stroke to disconcert Mère Blin, but the effect was just the opposite. She notes in the Chronicle :

"This gave great pleasure to me, for we were not without fear, when we considered the matter, of being crushed under the weight of the authority of the Bishop of Amiens, who had lost no time in justifying himself and in piling up his complaints against Mère Julie. His letter had arrived at Namur before her. . . ."

Later in the same day, a letter was handed to Mère Blin from the Vicar General of Amiens, which must have caused a whirlwind in her ideas and against which she indeed needed all her courage, all her confidence, in the simplicity and single-mindedness of Mère Julie.

"I find it impossible to keep silence," so the letter ran, "when I see the authority of the Bishop despised, set at naught, trampled under foot, by people who make a profession of piety. . . . If Mère Julie had shown you the letter she received from his Lordship, if she had repeated exactly the words which Monsieur Cottu had spoken to her in his name . . . you would have seen clearly that our Prelate did not order Mère Julie to leave unless 'she remained obstinate in withdrawing herself from his authority and refusing to recognize him as her superior. . . .' What especially underlines her disobedience is that she took Sœur Ciska with her, in spite of the Bishop's command that she should remain. . . . Mère Julie pretends to a mission from heaven to found an association and to govern it according to her own wishes. But where are the marks of

her mission? At what time has God said to his daughter:
'You will establish such an Order, you will rule it as you wish,
you will listen to neither Bishop nor Confessor except when
they show themselves reasonable in bowing to your wishes.
I give you absolute power over these young people who fight
under your standard, and whatsoever you do will be very well
done. . . .' Sœur Julie can speak of her revelations, but these
pretended revelations are merely the wiles of the devil to
seduce souls. When a person is without humility and simplicity, when she is tormented with a passion to command in
spite of her superiors, it is in vain that she claims to have real
revelations. . . . Therefore, Madame, if you look to your own
best interests you will take no pride in Mère Julie. . . . You
must choose between your Bishop and her. The choice is
yours. Religion, good sense, your happiness, your conscience
all point to what that choice should be. Make, therefore,
your choice, upon which will depend for you an eternity of
happiness or an eternity of pain. . . ."

It was a letter woven of appeal, of attack, of reference
to matters that could not be immediately tested, of little
flicks of something like sarcasm. That it was, however,
a sincere letter is shown by the fact that the first steps
towards recalling the Sisters to Amiens were taken by
this same Vicar General, to whom Mère Julie would
then be "la sainte Fille." Mère Blin's immediate
reaction to this letter was another of spirited defence,
in which all her deep devotion to her friend is gloriously
shown. We can imagine how the past gathered with a
certain wistfulness and glory in her eyes as she penned
these words:

"For twenty years she was deprived of the use of her limbs,
for twenty years she was racked with pain that seemed something alive in her body, for twenty years she lay on a bed which
God designed as a kind of Noviciate which prepared her for
the work to which He had destined her. Scarcely had her
condition improved a little than His call to found a Religious
Congregation became more urgent, more insistent. She experienced and manifested a great repugnance for this work,
finally when she saw nine or ten girls gathered round her while

she was still unable to walk, she cried out ceaselessly to heaven
that the use of her limbs might be restored to her, or that this
little group might disperse, since she was unable either to lead
or to train them in her suffering condition. We know how
these cries were answered, suddenly and entirely."

It is a beautiful letter, in which another of these
saintly friendships, earth's nearest approach to the conversation of the angels, is seen in all its loveliness.

When the Superior of the Seminary—"very tall, very
powerful in voice and in gesture "—arrived at the house
to make his protest, he was at the full tide of his eloquence. Mère Julie is under a delusion, you are all on
an evil way, you will not be blessed, you will not succeed, this is as sure as that you live, I ask God to strike
me dead this minute if I am attempting to deceive you.
It was the same series of arguments, the same mar-
shalling of texts, the same vehemence, only this time
strengthened with an appeal to the heavenly powers.
It was all very confusing. "Poor Mère Blin," she writes
of herself, "was under such pressure that she could
scarcely make a few words heard against the rush and
roar of this eloquence." Finally, she stood up with that
magnificently aristocratic calm with which she had so
often taken command of a situation, and said quietly:

"Monsieur, your manner of speaking to me prevents
me from having any confidence in what you are saying.
I beg you to pray to God for me."

Might he preach in the chapel now, as he had been
accustomed to do, he asked. Mère Blin did some quick
thinking and marshalled a few excuses for saying no.
"For he was too overwrought," she writes, "and he
could very easily have broken the spirit of the Sisters,
at least, he would have sown disquiet and fear among
them." Foiled in this, he went to the rooms of Madame
de Franssu, their great friend and helper who now lived
in a part of the convent, and poured forth a steady
stream of accusation against Mère Julie. He sent for

Mère Victoire, that she, too, might have the chance of being enlightened. Poor Madame Franssu was completely confused, but had the wisdom to suspend her judgment on the whole matter. She had the reward of her prudence, for very soon a letter came to her from Père Enfantin, " her angel," as she called him, the priest who had advised her to come and live with the Sisters, the priest who had been the instrument in the cure of Julie Billiart. In the thought of seeing him soon, she found peace.

The next bubble in the cauldron of confusion was Mère Victoire's open declaration of her intention to remain in Amiens. M. de Sambucy was in a mood to mount the house-tops and shout the glory of " the future house of Amiens, which he now believed he could establish on a better footing than the old, and the finance of which, he was confident, would come from Madame de Franssu." Mère Victoire announced her decision, with tears, to Mère Blin.

" I grieve bitterly," she said, "because I feel that I am being forced. I see that Mère Julie's reasons are good—but I am being forced into a way I would not choose."

This was indeed true, for, as Mère Blin records, "they went so far as to tell her that, if she departed, they would have her brought back by the police; moreover, that her departure would make any reconciliation between Mère Julie and the Bishop utterly impossible, while her decision to remain would hasten that reconciliation. . . ." It was a time for clear thinking and heroic tenacity, and Mère Victoire was still youthful and far from the stuff of which heroines are made. M. de Sambucy's success with Madame de Franssu was not quite as immediate as he would have wished. However, he succeeded in sowing sufficient confusion to cause her to take the control of her money out of Mère Julie's hand and deposit it, until matters should clear a little, and especially, perhaps, until she should have discussed the whole affair with Père Enfantin.

With Mère Blin, M. de Sambucy felt he was making no progress. He had skilfully got her out of the house on pretext of an urgent summons from the Bishop, while he harangued the Sisters with threats of hell fire and all the terrors of bell, book and candle. But he was now dealing with one who was well able to see through his ruses. Her first greeting to him after this incident was:

"Well, mon Père. So it was your good pleasure the other day to indulge in a little juggling at my expense."

He muttered a few incoherencies, and then began, characteristically, to lay down the law about something else. This time it was the chapel. The tabernacle must not be removed, the Bishop would not hear of that, indeed the Commissioner of Police would be called in if she attempted to do so. "Mère Blin knew very well," she comments, "that these were tactics for frightening the children, since the Commissioner would find nothing to concern him in the whole affair." She answered with her usual calm firmness:

"Out of respect for his Lordship, it will not be removed. But I should like to make it very clear to you, Monsieur de Sambucy, that the community will not renounce any of its rights."

"In spite of this, however," Mère Blin goes on to comment, "the cry, so to speak, of 'Thieves, thieves' was ceaselessly chorused for some church ornament or some trifle which had been the gift of Madame de Franssu and which Mère Julie had taken with her. And yet," she continues with a delightfully ironical smile behind the page, "they must have considered these thefts well worthy of pardon, since Monsieur de Sambucy himself begged Madame de Franssu to ask Mère Julie to leave a ciborium, donated by her."

On January 31st, 1809, six Sisters departed for

Namur, leaving only Sœur Angelique Sachy with Mère Blin to attend to the rest of the affairs. M. de Sambucy, having now no subjects, was forced to appoint one of the boarders as portress, with instructions to give a precise account to Mère Victoire of all who called to see Mère Blin. The house was now thoroughly divided against itself, Mère Blin and Sœur Angelique at one table, Mère Victoire and the boarder at the other, for they were now the "old" and the "new" community. Great efforts were made to win over Sœur Angelique. Mère Victoire, who seems to have quickly forgotten her tears and her protestations, frequently whispered in the young Sister's ear: "Alas, poor Sister, you scarcely know what awaits you. . . ."

The last few days were taken up for Mère Blin with the sale of those things which she could not take with her. When she obtained a valuation of the goods, she went to M. de Sambucy and offered him an option on them, since he was to be head of the house now. He seems to have rejected the offer in a high-handed manner, saying that the Bishop had forbidden him to buy anything. He had the idea that Mère Blin would leave a considerable amount in the house anyhow, and he was utterly amazed when she did not. Always anxious to sharpen his case against Mère Julie, he said to Mère Blin:

"If you were acting on your own conviction, you would take a kinder decision in the matter."

"I am acting on my own conviction," she answered, seeing immediately the implication of his words, "for there is no question of harshness here, but merely a question of justice."

And M. de Sambucy stormed off, to write another letter to the Bishop of Namur, in which truth was woven gaily in and out with hurt pride and heated misrepresentation.

Some days before her departure from Amiens, Mère

L

Blin sent on by road the goods and chattels which had
been bought by her and would be needed at the new
Mother house at Namur. The rest she sold to two or
three persons after one of the workmen in the house
had estimated their value. All was done quietly and in
an orderly manner. Unfortunately a few women from
the town came into the court in the afternoon to buy
some of the household utensils and, after the fashion
of women of their type, shouted and made a disturbance. This was as displeasing to Mère Blin as to Mère
Victoire, but with minds as poisoned as were those of
M. de Sambucy and his protégée the regrettable incident was turned to good account in their persecution
of Mère Julie.

M. de Sambucy had, in his usual high-handed
manner and without consulting Madame Barat, in-
stalled as Superior of the Amiens house Sœur Marie
Prévost, one of the Ladies of the Sacred Heart. Very
shortly after Mère Blin's departure, he sent Sœur Marie
Prévost to Montdidier with the avowed object of turning the Sisters there against Mère Julie. A perfectly
false account of the sale was given them: it was said to
have taken place on a Sunday, to have been the cause
of great scandal and so on. The blame was laid upon
Julie, all was attributed to the bad training she had
given her daughters. But the Montidier Sisters were
proof against lies and distorted stories; neither fair
words nor threats could wrest them from Mère Julie
and their first vocation. They wrote letter after letter
to their Mother assuring her of their undying loyalty
and love.

Two letters arrived at Namur testifying to the general
confusion. One was from the Bishop of Amiens, rejoicing that at least the houses of the diocese were remaining faithful to him: the other was from M. de Sambucy
complaining that Mère Julie had seduced the Sisters
of Montdidier from their episcopal allegiance. While

they were writing these letters, Mère Blin was fixing the last luggage on the cart.   It was a heavy load, so heavy indeed that they scarcely succeeded in getting on their way before the vehicle broke down.   It was one of those last-minute vexations with which we are all familiar. But it was set right and they continued their journey.

Later, she would pen her final verdict on it all. " The leaders of the Amiens House had treated rigorously and shackled the instrument chosen by Providence, and therefore this house deserved to lose its title of Mother house, its title of daughter house and even its existence. By opening its doors to this rejected family and receiving them into its bosom, the Namur house deserved to succeed to this title."   In that sentence was born the title splendidly honoured by one of the finest teaching Congregations in the Church to-day—The Institute of Sisters of Notre Dame de Namur.

Her face was set for Namur : and as she sat in that conveyance and watched the last houses of the town giving place to fields and the open country spaces, a great surge of thankfulness and relief must have gone through her, the relief a person feels whose face and body have been tangled in clinging, clammy cobwebs ceaselessly spun about her, and who emerges into the sunshine and feels the wind clean in her face.

CHAPTER ELEVEN

THE UNRAVELLING

WITH the dust of their journey upon them and its exhaustion heavy in their eyes, Mère Julie and her companions, reinforced by Sœur Jeanne Godelle and her group who, thanks to a more intelligent conductor, had overtaken the first carriage just outside Namur, drew up outside the Bishop's residence. And when Mère Julie approached the Bishop, she was met with a welcome as icy as the frost and sleet through which she had just passed. For the Bishop was greatly troubled by the letters of M. de Sambucy.

"I did not ask for you," he greeted her. "Neither did I counsel the foolhardy displacement of an entire community in the depth of winter. . . . Walk cautiously, Ma Sœur, for people favoured with revelations have before now been damned for their lack of obedience. Besides, you have given me no warning of your coming."

"Pardon me, Your Lordship," she answered, "Mère Blin has written to you."

"Her letter was previous to all this."

"Look at the date, My Lord," she pleaded, "pray look at the date."

The letter was found and the matter settled to the Bishop's satisfaction. A long two hours of questioning followed, but it became more and more obvious to the good Bishop that he was placing the virtue of Simplicity incarnate in the dock, for twistings and duplicity. At the end of the interview, he pronounced himself satisfied, and welcomed her with the warmth which only repeated misrepresentations in high places had caused him to hold in check. These letters continued to come, more and more abundantly, from M. de Sambucy, but they now did no harm except to the person who wrote them. For M. de Sambucy's influence was ebbing fast, and the very frequency and frantic quality of his letters testified to this.

The poverty of the Sisters at Namur is reminiscent of student life in thirteenth-century Paris. We are told, as illustrating the poverty of these men, that they often had but one cloak between two, so that one had to remain in his garret while the other attended the schools. There is an interesting echo of this in one of the first comments Mère Blin makes on the early months in Namur.

"The Bishop," she writes, "had promised that as soon as Mère Blin should arrive, he would permit Holy Mass to be celebrated in the chapel. However, he decided to defer this until April 21st, so that he himself might be the celebrant. Until then the Sisters went to the parish church, and this entailed a great deal of inconvenience, since they had few veils and were obliged to go out by turns."

It is pleasing to notice such an echo from the story of the great, pulsating movement of medieval intellectualism, in another movement not unworthy of its great scope and its burning enthusiasm.

Namur had a welcome for them, for the face of Namur softened at the name "Exiles." Here Julienne de Mont Cornillon had found rest for her heart, wearied by her struggle to exalt her Eucharistic Lord. And now another exile had come to the city of exiles, not broken, not wearied, but full of energy to dig deep and to build high.

The scarcity of veils was far from being the only thing lacking to the smooth functioning of convent life, "for," notes Mère Blin, "the whole place was unsuitable, the houses, courts, garden, cellars and outhouses being in a state of incredible chaos." The Sisters set to work with a will; Mère Julie was foremost among them, but soon an urgent call came which caused her to abandon her brush and duster and set off immediately for St.-Nicolas.

The house at St.-Nicolas was too small, another must be found, said the urgent message: but much more than that, there was a bug scare, than which there is nothing quite so potent in spreading panic among parents. "In spite of this alarm," the note reads, with a certain humour, "we have succeeded in finding only two." They must indeed have been two super specimens of the genus, for the parents were certainly coming to take away their children!

The immediate result for Mère Julie was that she was brought face to face with the Bishop of Ghent somewhat sooner than she had expected. M. de Sambucy had boasted of his influence with this Bishop, and had assured Mère Julie that she would find no quarter there. To her amazement, however, she was received with cordiality, and when his Lordship had shown her to a seat with great courtesy, he asked her smilingly:

"Well, let me have the full story of the Amiens affair."

He did not have the full story, for, as Mère Blin remarks, Mère Julie's details were first inspected by her charity, so that many things remained untold. However, the Bishop was not unaware of this, and he assured her warmly that a glowing welcome awaited every Sister of Notre Dame in his diocese. He made good his warmth by sending very soon to have the community of St.-Nicolas removed to the house of the Sœurs de la Charité in Ghent, while some provision was being made for them. Happily another house was soon found.

The events which led up to this removal from St.-Nicolas quicken the tempo of the narrative in the early chronicles. The Bishop of Ghent had accompanied Mère Julie on a visit of inspection, and he had been appalled by the insanitary conditions of the place. He remonstrated with the civil authorities, but they shared the prejudice of the people against religious who were Frenchwomen, and considered dripping walls and fever conditions ideal for such as they.

"Shake the dust of this town from off your feet," the Bishop counselled her as they parted. "If St.-Nicolas continues to treat you in such an ugly way, come to Ghent and settle there, for I must have you in my diocese."

She was very grateful to him, and the glow of his recent words were still hearteningly with her:

"You are not intended to be shut up in one diocese; no, Mère Julie, your vocation is to go all over the world."

When the Bishop told Julie to remove the Sisters "without delay," he did not reckon on her taking him quite so literally. But there was a forthrightness about her which caused action to follow hard on decision, and so, very soon, a carriage with the Sisters and their belongings was moving away from the draughty, crumbling, insanitary house at St.-Nicolas. The mood of the people was ugly. A crowd surrounded the carriage on its way out of the town, shouting insults and blasphemies at the Sisters who had spent every moment of two years in giving a full measure of loving service. With harsh words beating about them and angry faces raised to them, they looked to their Mother, sitting placidly in their midst. She smiled on them, and her eyes brimmed with joy. There was courage in the smile, an undaunted bravery in the joy-brimmed eyes that lifted their minds to another scene. For she told them with her voice, with her eyes, with her smile, that it was their joy to be allowed thus to mirror a moment in the life of their Master.

Julie's action had been hastened by the expiration of the lease of the house: but the Bishop had not forgotten about this, and besides, had not reckoned on Mère Julie being so prompt in action. He was therefore far from pleased to have these Sisters suddenly brought to his door, presenting him with a pressing problem for the solving of which he was wholly unprepared. However, room was found for them in the convent of the Sisters of Charity, where two rooms and a small kitchen were placed at their disposal. Here again we come on one of those early vignettes, a family group, so to speak, which catches and enshrines a moment of difficulty, of courage, of joy in the Cross, and fixes it for all time as an inspiration to those whose vows are made in the name of Notre Dame.

They had no furniture, for that in St.-Nicolas had belonged to the people and had been left there. "We were seven," writes Julie, "and there were four beds." Clothes were spread on the floor to make other beds, and "a few faggots found in the corner served as pillows." They sat down to eat a supper of dry bread. Having no candle, they were groping in the darkness, settling themselves as best they could, when "a knock came to the door, and the director of the hospice appeared with his servant, bringing a lamp and a jug of beer." It is good, in a blasé world, to think of the simple joy and merriment with which they accepted these gifts: to picture them sitting on the floor about the lamp and finding the bread not nearly so dry now that the jug passed joyfully from hand to hand. This bread had to last so long that green patches of mould covered it: "But," says Sœur Marie Steenhaut in her Chronicle, "Mère Julie used to bless it and it never did us any harm." "To-day," writes Julie to Mère Blin, "I set up our kitchen with fourteen pence. That was good buying, was it not? We have bread, salt and butter, and we are buying potatoes. We are the happiest people in all the city of Ghent. Of the six lois which I brought away with me, I still have five. I believe God, like a good Father, must multiply them in my purse." Details like these are the Fioretti of Notre Dame, filling the dawn with the sweet odour of courage and of joy. It were well that the followers of Julie Billiart in every age should inhale that sweet odour and know the renewal of spirit it can bring.

Perhaps we are too apt to think of the Foundress of a Religious Order in the Church as a mighty soul breathing on the earth and finding new branches of her movement, all shining, complete and wanting for nothing, in the places where she has breathed. This is, to some extent, the inner truth, for it is the spirit that quickeneth, the bricks and mortar of themselves being profitless. But, in the field of practicalities, the foundation of each house is a matter of hard work, of courage to face a host of difficulties, patience to attend to a swarming mass of detail. We find all this in Mère Julie's search for a house in Ghent, as we turn over the pages of her letters to Mère Blin from "the two rooms and a kitchen." To-morrow, she says, she cannot write, for she must "beat the town for a house." The energy with which the child Julie had set off for a strange town to seek a buyer for her father's goods remained with her as a woman, so we can well imagine the tireless energy hidden in that word "beat." There seemed little hope of getting a house in Ghent, but, in the midst of her search, she received an offer of a house in the parish of St. Pierre. There was still no house to be got in Ghent, when Monseigneur de Broglie, Bishop of Ghent, summoned Julie and expressed his deep desire that a house should be established at the important country town of St. Gilles. "I am not like the Bishop of Amiens," he said to her. "So far from wishing to

send you away, I am most anxious to have many of
your houses in my diocese." This must indeed have
come as consoling balm to Julie in the midst of cares
that were piling up daily about her. She has many
decisions to make. "I am dragged about on all sides,"
she whispers in a letter to Mère Blin.

One day somebody mentioned an old Abbey in
another part of Ghent which, from the sixteenth century till its recent suppression, had been a convent of
Cistercian nuns. Julie made immediate enquiries and
learned that it was in the temporary possession of a
gentleman of Ghent, to whom it had been sold "on
condition that the Sisters should be allowed to buy it
back if they were ever able to reconstitute their scat-
tered community." She lost no time in going to see the
place, and was grieved to see that the church, which
had so often echoed with the beauty of the Psalms and
been made rich with the riches of Cistercian prayer,
had been turned, now into a barn, now into a powder
magazine, now into a shelter for beasts. It would be
good to bring her active work for souls to this place
steeped in prayer and praise, she must have mused as
she stood in the Abbey: it would serve as a living
reminder to her Sisters of that truth she impressed on
them at all times—that all spiritual activity must be
fed from the strength of prayer, that they must "grapple
themselves to the good God," that they must be "soaked
in God." Of the Cistercian Sisters there remained but
two, and these laughed at the quaintly dressed peasant-
woman who came seeking their Abbey. "What! " they
exclaimed to Monsieur Lemaire, who had been negotiat-
ing the business, "is that the person? " and, we are told,
one of them burst out laughing. Julie Billiart was
used to being laughed at, scoffed at, jeered at, but her
only interest in laughs, scoffs or jeers was as possible
indications of the Will of God. Monsieur Lemaire
explained a few things to them; they were old ladies,

and possibly a little reluctant to accept the new movement, but they soon learned to appreciate Mère Julie,
and the Abbey was made over to her in the year 1810.

What all this involved for the Foundress is admirably
outlined by one of her biographers, who, dealing with
the foundation at St. Pierre, writes:

"Her heart bounded with joy at the sight of the good to
be done amongst the poor of that district, and she writes
exultingly to her friend at Namur of the one hundred and
thirty-two children who at once poured into the school. There
are as many poor in the place as there are stones; she
does not know how the good Sisters will be able to get
through all the work they have before them. But the good
God is very good! She herself has been trotting about all
the morning buying this article or that for the modest *ménage*
of the Rue des Femmes: a stove, a saucepan, a gridiron, all
sorts. Mère Blin will wonder where all the money comes from.
Well, for one thing she takes care to get cheap things, though
sometimes she has to hunt a long time before finding them.
And then, too, somehow or other, she cannot quite understand
how, she always finds a few crowns in her pocket."

Yes, collecting "a stove, a saucepan, a gridiron" can
find its place in the founding of an Institute.

And meantime, what of M. de Sambucy and affairs
at Amiens? He comes again into our story at this
point, no longer repentant but with the violence we
have learnt to expect from him. On his own initiative
he wrote to the Bishop of Ghent, giving him his own
version of the Amiens difficulties, and informing him
of the danger he was running by giving authority to
the headstrong and illusion-blinded Julie Billiart: the
Bishop of Amiens, he went on, had now happily purged
Notre Dame of her bad spirit, the houses under his
jurisdiction could breathe freely, and moreover, the
Mother-house of Amiens was in a position to supply
the different dioceses with Sisters of Notre Dame "to
replace those of Sœur Julie." But the man he was

addressing was Maurice-Jean de Broglie, son of Victor
Francis, Duke of Broglie and Marshal of France, and he
was not used to being addressed arrogantly or having
his intelligence underrated by someone who obviously
thought him incapable of seeing through a tissue of
inconsistencies and misrepresentations. He decided it
was time that this persistent meddler should be put in
his place. Monseigneur de Broglie took up his pen
and, with the very first sentence he wrote, he set in
motion the reaction against M. de Sambucy which was
to lead to his rapid eclipse and his final disgrace. It is
a dry-pointed, logical letter, with now and then a calculated stern reproof laid on in the letter like a finger
of ice. Anyone less headstrong that M. de Sambucy
would have known immediately that his lease of fault-
finding and misrepresentation was up.

"GHENT, *June 25th, 1809.*
"You are very young, Sir, to set yourself up, as you do, to
judge, or rather to censure the actions of a Bishop. Salvien,
St. Jerome and St. Bernard were called in their time the Masters
of the Bishops, but between them and you there is, you will
allow, some difference. I had intended to give no answer to
your letters about Sister Julie, but your last to M. le Surre
prevents me from following this plan. If you have a copy of
that letter, read it over again, and I hope the expressions used
with regard to myself will strike you as very unbecoming. I
will not follow the maze of your remarks; I will merely observe
that:
"1. It is very strange that you should give so much praise
to the Bishop of Namur, who has done so much more than
the Bishop of Ghent, who has received at Namur, to use your
own expression, 'the Superior and religious emigrants from
Amiens,' who has occupied himself with their establishment
in his city, and has spent whole hours in their convent after
offering the Holy Sacrifice there; while the Bishop of Ghent has
confined himself to allowing the removal into another town
of a community which already existed at St.-Nicolas under his
predecessor. It is not I, but they, who have decided not to
adhere to the changes made in the Constitutions at Amiens
and at Montdidier, and who have remained attached to the

same Superior and the same Rule as before. Notwithstanding this, you dare to say: 'The excellent Bishop of Namur has treated of this with the Bishop of Amiens and myself in so frank and loyal a manner that we have only to congratulate ourselves on our correspondence with him.' This implies the contrary for me, so that I am neither frank nor loyal. M. de Sambucy, I forgive you this language, but do not use it again, and remember to whom you write, and of whom you speak. The Bishop of Amiens has not written a line to me on the subject; if he had, I should have done myself the honour of writing to him in all frankness and loyalty, for I never act otherwise.

"2. You add: 'The Bishop of Namur approves, it is true, of a Superior-General, but this point is never opposed to the wishes of the majority of the Bishops.' One would suppose that you were the confidant of 'the majority of the Bishops.' The Bishop of Amiens will not hear of a Superior-General. The Bishop of Namur wishes for one. And yet, if I am to believe you, these two are in perfect harmony. And the Bishop of Ghent, who has nothing to do with all this, who has done no more than keep in his diocese the nuns established by his predecessor, is the only person in the wrong. You wanted me to take part with the Bishop of Amiens against the Bishop of Namur. You are really very strange. Could I carry moderation further than to send you word I would conform to whatever my two colleagues decided? The Bishop of Amiens and you (for you consider yourselves two in one mind) do not want a Superior-General, there are only local Superiors. What in that case is to prevent Sister Julie from being Superior in the house that exists in the diocese of Ghent?

"3. If the Bishop of Namur is right in holding to a Superior-General, Sister Julie was that Superior before the changes introduced, under your direction, into this Association. And why may I not incline towards the opinion of one of my colleagues rather than that of another?

"4. The truth of all this is, that your changes have not had the success you hoped for, and yet you do not repent of having made them. As for me, I keep what my predecessors left me. I leave these nuns under the same rules they came with, and as you will not have a Superior-General, you cannot find fault with a Convent governed by a particular Superior.

"5. You say I owe nothing to the Bishop of Namur. I may tell you that both before the Revolution and since, I have been much more intimate with him than with the Bishop of

Amiens, whom I scarcely know at all. I like and esteem both these respected colleagues, but why should I blame what the Bishop of Namur does, in order to please the Bishop of Amiens? And if, while he received all the emigrant nuns, I had not kept them in my diocese, should I not have appeared to censure what my colleague did?

" 6. You tell me these nuns belong to the Bishop of Amiens. They came into my diocese under my predecessor. As neither you nor your Bishop will have a Superior-General, theirs cannot be considered by you as a true Congregation, but only as consisting of isolated communities. Every Bishop has equal right and jurisdiction over all such associations existing in his diocese, for, properly speaking, we have now no real religious Orders, and, above all, we have no communities of nuns exempt from episcopal jurisdiction.

" 7. You maintain ' that it would be very easy for me to conciliate the parties.' No one has asked me to do that, and how could there be an agreement between one Bishop who wants changes in this Congregation, and another who receives the emigrant nuns in his diocese? Besides ' these two respected Bishops have had only to congratulate themselves on their correspondence regarding this business.' As they are completely in harmony, what need is there to conciliate those who agree so happily?

" 8. Before concluding, I cannot pass over in silence your saying now that there are thirteen nuns on your side, instead of two, according to the Bishop of Amiens, and six, according to your note. It would have been more straightforward to say thirteen from the first, but it did not, seemingly, suit you at that time. You add, that four of these new subjects have had a long trial with the Ladies of the Sacred Heart, and were formed under your supervision for the new Institute; which meant that long before this reform of yours, you were preparing in another Congregation the means of putting an end to that of Sister Julie. Is this frankness and loyalty? The interest I take in you prompts me to advise you not to judge and blame a Bishop, and not to meddle with so many matters. For my part, I have kept what I found, and I have left things as they were.

"Accept, Sir, the assurance of my sincere attachment,

"MAURICE, BISHOP OF GHENT."

One phrase stands out coldly: " The truth of all this

THE CHILDREN OF THE POOR WERE THE BEST-BELOVED
OF JULIE'S FLOCK

is that your changes have not had the success you hoped for, and yet you do not repent of having made them." This stubborn attitude of M. de Sambucy, this unrepentant recognition of crumbling plans, give the pulse of the situation at Amiens. When he found himself with a free hand there, he transferred four novices from the Ladies of the Sacred Heart to the Notre Dame house, and appointed one of them, Marie Elizabeth Prévost, as Superior. Mère Victoire's star had dimmed, and her angelic lustre had lost a lot of its shimmer in the eyes of Monsieur: she made difficulties for the new Superior, and Monsieur sent her off, in something like disgrace, to Rubempré. He was keeping up a ceaseless assault on the constancy of Montdidier. . . . The Superior, Sœur Marie Caroline, was summoned to Amiens, and detained there for several days, during which time she was plied with exhortations both by the Bishop and M. de Sambucy to sever herself and her convent from Julie Billiart. But Montdidier stood firm.

The same tactics were tried with Sœur Catherine Daulee, Superior of the house at Ghent. "God has seen fit," M. de Sambucy wrote to her, "to effect a separation, and Mère Julie is now at Namur with almost all her daughters. I am confident, however, you will remain united with the house of Amiens." The reply was as pointed as that of the Bishop of Ghent. It read:

"Monsieur, I have the honour to tell you that I no longer recognize Amiens as the cradle of my Order if the government which God had put in Mère Julie's hands is to be taken away from her. . . . It is useless to speak to me of rules, or to make any other proposals to me; I have one intention only, which is, *to follow my Mother, to follow my Mother.* . . ."

The voice of determined opposition was loud about M. de Sambucy, and he was beginning to feel his own voice rather ineffective against it. But the Sisters had a very trying time indeed, until eventually their heroic constancy won the day and permission was given to the Sisters at Montdidier to join Mère Julie in Belgium. At this point in the Chronicle we come on another of those lovely touches of the courtesy of God which delight us in the stories of saints. The Sisters of Montdidier were wandering in the streets of Plessier-sur-St.-Just, waiting for a carriage to Belgium. They turned a corner, and found themselves in the arms of that Mother whom they had so longed to see. "The joy of the meeting," says Mère Blin, "was indescribable." Mère Julie had come on a stray bit of business, and had no suspicion of any of her daughters being there, much less those of Montdidier, whom prudence would have prevented her from visiting.

As time went on, the Namur foundation prospered visibly, whereas the house at Amiens from which Mère Julie had been banished seemed on the point of extinction. This situation opened the eyes of the Bishop. He began to be alive to many things, and when he came alive, the swing of the pendulum was a decided one indeed. It swung against M. de Sambucy with all the force of reaction to a hundred rash schemes, the failure of which seemed gathered up in one great fact—the death of a fine religious movement in the heart of Amiens. The Bishop began to ask many questions, to question many facts which before had passed muster under the name of M. de Sambucy. The result was inevitable. The Bishop and his Council realized at long last that they had put far too much confidence in him and far too little in Mère Julie. The pendulum swung full circle: M. de Sambucy was banished from the diocese and Mère Julie recalled. Père Sellier was charged by his Lordship with making the first advances. In a letter dated September, 1812, he informed Mère Julie that he had undertaken to speak to the Vicar General and warn him that, if the Amiens house was to survive, it was high time the Foundress was recalled.

To his utter surprise, the Vicar General needed no persuasion, but exclaimed: "It is more than time. We have been deceived, yes, thoroughly deceived. But do you think she will return to us?" "I am sure she will," Père Sellier had replied.

Soon a letter was on its way to Julie from the Vicar General. She received it, but delayed her reply. Another letter came almost immediately, this time from the Bishop himself.

"AMIENS, *October 23rd, 1812.*

"Monsieur Sellier has undertaken, my dear daughter, to express to you the desire I have to see you back at Amiens, in order to take up again the government of the Sisters of Notre Dame in my diocese, which you left in consequence of an error caused by one whom I believed I could trust. Now, more enlightened, I am not afraid to own to you that I have been deceived in your regard. I urge you then, my dear daughter, to return as soon as possible, if not to fix yourself here at once, at least to make the arrangements which the new order of things will necessitate. You may depend upon the most cordial welcome from Sœur Marie (Prévost) and her companions, who will be enchanted to submit to your authority, as they have unanimously assured me."

It was a very gratifying letter, but there was one lack in it which the wary eye of Julie did not miss. No mention was made of her status of Mother General. She wrote hinting at this and suggesting a clarification of his attitude towards her. There was something in the steady common sense of Julie which made her cautious of what might very well be the mood of a moment. It is significant that the Bishop replied immediately:

"Either I have explained myself badly, my dear Daughter, or you must quite have misunderstood me. It is in nowise my design to make you quit Namur and establish yourself at Amiens; but looking on yourself as the Superior-General of your Institute, I would simply ask you to come here to visit your convent, and to make all the reforms in it you think advisable, so that the same spirit may reign amongst you all. . . ."

M

In addition to this, on November 16th, the Bishop sent to Mère Julie an official document under his sign and seal declaring his recognition of her position as Mother General of all the Houses of Notre Dame in his diocese and according her all the powers, rights and privileges granted to her by his fellow Bishops, in whose dioceses the Sisters of Notre Dame were established.

Julie no longer hesitated. She set off at once for Amiens with mixed feelings. She was secretly convinced that the reconciliation would not be a success: but the Bishop was insistent, her nuns were confident; above all there had come a letter from the Sisters in Amiens which Julie herself described as "*à cor et à cri,*" and all this she thought to be a clear indication of God's Will.

On the 18th November, 1812, she arrived at Amiens and went immediately to the Bishop's residence, where she was received with a warmth in which there was the sincerest of sincere attempts to blot out the chilling moments of the past. The sorely tried members of the Amiens community were visibly rejoiced to have their Mother back. She found the house in an insolvent condition, without resources of any kind. There were fourteen Sisters and ten boarders who were an added expense since they paid no fees. Mère Julie did not let the grass grow under her feet. She obtained the Bishop's consent to let the Faubourg Noyon to the nephew of the Curé of Amiens Cathedral and settle the Sisters in a smaller house. She writes playfully to Mère Blin:

"People are offering me houses on all sides for forty to sixty thousand francs: and I am running all over the town to find one for nothing! It is your name, my dear, which gives me this great reputation. The immediate need is to pay the debts. . . . I wait for God to show us what is best to do."

After a very long search, accommodation was found

for some of the Sisters in an old Convent in the grounds
of which a cotton factory had been built. The directors
of this factory gave them the rooms in the Convent
free and agreed to pay them 300 francs if they would
undertake the religious instruction of the factory girls.
Mère Julie closed with this offer, and she also accepted
the proposal of the Count de Renneville to establish
two or three Sisters, to whom he guaranteed a small
income, in the school house of Renneville, a village
about six miles from Amiens. Sœur Marie Henocque
was made Superior of this little foundation which from
the outset counted as many as forty day-scholars and
seven boarders.

The Bishop warmly approved of the steps taken by
Mère Julie to place things on a better footing and
enable the Sisters to pay off some of their debts. A
letter from him to his colleague in Namur shows how
completely Mère Julie has been rehabilitated, both with
the ecclesiastical authorities and with the Community
of the Amiens Convent.

" My Lord,
        " I cannot do otherwise than own to you that I have had
to reproach myself exceedingly for having followed the per-
nicious advice that was given me, inducing me to send the good
Mère Julie out of my diocese. The harm done by her departure was so serious that I found myself on the point of losing
several precious institutions if I had not hastened to recall
her, and if you, on your side, had not urged her to yield to my
pressing entreaties. Her return has filled me with joy, and I
have been as much touched as pleased by the reception she has
met with from her former community, and by the holy eager-
ness with which the Superior whom I had appointed there
resigned her post, protesting to Mère Julie that she did so
with all her heart, being only too happy to live henceforward
in dependence and as the last of her Sisters. All is not yet
definitely settled. But I have begun the work by recognizing
Mère Julie as Superior-General of her Congregation. I have
forwarded to her the Act of her nomination, not forgetting her
title of Foundress, and I now indulge a well-grounded hope

that, under the direction of this excellent religious, her Congregation will begin a new life in my diocese. Thus, my Lord, it is to you, after God, that I shall be beholden for the great good which Providence is about to work through her instrumentality. Accept the assurance of the sincere and respectful attachment with which I am, my Lord,

"Your most humble and obedient servant,
" J.-Fr., Bishop of Amiens."

But Mère Julie did not share his high hopes. Without finding in the community grave defects, she felt at every turn that its spirit was different from that which she had tried to form in her daughters. She writes to Mère Blin:

"We have a difficult work in hand; I want your prayers, and many of them. When on entering the house, as I told you, I met our dear Jesus fleeing from Amiens, He saw very well what my repugnance was. . . . My God, Thou wilt deliver us, if it please Thee."

Early in December, seeing that matters were provisionally arranged, she returned to Namur. It would seem as if in the designs of God the sole aim of this visit to Amiens had been her own justification, for hardly had she left there than letter after letter came from Sr. Marie Prévost telling her of new troubles. To the Foundress they looked like couriers of Providence announcing its dissolution.

The administrators of the factory withdrew the house and the promised fees. The gentleman who had rented the former Convent asked to be released from his engagement, as he had found a more convenient residence. Finally Sr. Marie Prévost announced that she desired to return to her first religious home with the Ladies of the Sacred Heart. Mère Julie saw in all this a clear manifestation of the Will of God. She wrote to the Vicar General, and, after acquainting him with the facts, pointed out the impossibility of maintaining a community at Amiens under the circumstances, and asked to have it suppressed by diocesan authority. The Bishop gave his consent, the house was dissolved, and Mère Julie settled the Sisters who wished to follow her in Namur or in one of the secondary houses. The dissolution of the remaining houses in France followed close upon that of Amiens.

In the light of these events, the words of Julie already quoted, "I met our dear Jesus fleeing from Amiens," are full of significance for our story. As Julie approached the door of the Amiens house to re-enter the home from which she had been expelled, the figure of Christ laden with His Cross emerged from the shadows of the porch and came to meet her. Amazed at this vision, she stood still, like one of the group of women who stood by the wayside to offer Him their silent tears. Moving away from the Convent, He fixed pain-filled eyes upon her and said:

"Look at Me, and follow Me: I am the Way, the Truth and the Life."

In a moment the vision was gone. She continued towards the house. Few would know of this, until the process of Beatification would bring forth such wonders, for if there was one thing about which this most simple and candid of women was close and secretive, it was the supernatural favours with which she was favoured by God.

It is interesting to speculate on the significance of this vision. Perhaps it was Christ's underlining of the fact that, in this moment of triumphant vindication, her glory must still be in the Cross of Christ. Perhaps, also, it was Christ the Bridegroom coming to her, recognizing the beauty of her wedding-garment wrought of pain: Christ, the Spouse of the Canticle, His lips "as lilies dropping liquid myrrh."

The vision of the image in which she had shaped her soul, meeting her.

CHAPTER TWELVE

"FOR THEY SHALL POSSESS. . . ."

WHEN searching for the character of Julie
Billiart in the teeming Chronicle which
records the early Foundations of the Congregation of Notre Dame, two outstanding qualities
reveal themselves: strength and tenderness. Her
strength and courage struck all who had anything to
do with her. To fear difficulty or danger, to shrink
from hardships or fatigue, were things impossible to
her. Yet there was no rigidity of harshness in Julie's
strength and energy; she was strong as are God's winds
and waters, which are also the gentlest of His creatures.

The single fact that between the years 1806 and 1816
she made over one hundred and twenty journeys, many
of them extremely long and always under very difficult
travelling conditions, is sufficient testimony to her
courageous endurance and enterprise. On one of these
journeys we find a scene of some excitement: Passing
through a little town called Fleurus, she was surrounded
by children who crowded round, vying with each other
to obtain a better view. She spoke pleasantly to them,
all unconscious of the curiosity her black habit and her
religious air were arousing. . . . A gendarme, three-
quarters drunk, pushed through the children and
demanded her passport. She replied simply that she
had none. "Very well, Madame," he stammered, "you
will go to prison." As she saw he was incapable of
listening to reason, she followed him to the Mayor.
Things would have gone badly with her had not the
good God brought to her mind a letter she had in

her pocket from the Archbishop of Bordeaux. She presented this and, with many apologies, the Mayor allowed her to continue her journey.

Another time, in 1810, it was question of a very difficult and anxious journey from Amiens to Ghent. She had succeeded at last in obtaining from M. de Sambucy a sum of money belonging to Mère Blin of which he had long been in possession. With a gesture worthy of his character, he had given her the 10,400 francs in coin, and she was compelled to travel in a coach with two heavy and conspicuous baskets into which she had poured the money. The bigger basket she put between her legs and the smaller one she kept on her knee. When the other passengers alighted for a meal, she sat on in the coach guarding her precious baskets. But at nightfall there was nothing for it but to descend and seek shelter in the inn for the night. Her heavy basket evoked much comment and no little suspicion. At one moment the asmosphere was so tense that Mère Julie offered to God the sacrifice of her life and prepared for death! Nor were her troubles at an end when she reached Ghent, for the coach stop was at a considerable distance from the Convent, and the baskets had to be got there! Fortunately some little girls from one of our schools saw Mère Julie and ran to the Convent at her request to get help for her. A Sister was soon on the spot, lifted the burden, puffed and panted, struggled on manfully, Mère Julie helping her as best she could. Finally neither could go a step further and dropped their baskets at the door of a house. By God's providence, it was the house of Monsieur Lemaire, a great friend of the Sisters, and Mère Julie's troubles were over for that day.

Another time she is making a journey with a farmer in a small cart, his great body spread over the seat, crushing her against the side, his talk all of land and crops and ways of making money, for "his mind," says

Mère Blin, "was as refined as his body!" Mère Julie wished to see Madame de Franssu at Amiens, but did not think it wise to visit the house from which she had been expelled. She sent a note by the farmer, and " when he was in the convent, Mère Victoire recognized him and ran forward asking eagerly: 'Have you any news of Mère Julie? Where is she?' 'She is here,' he answered. Then Mère Victoire, in a rapture of joy, raised her hands to heaven, exclaiming that God had sent him. She learned Mère Julie's whereabouts and rushed to her. She threw herself on her knees, wept, laughed, wept, begged for pardon, all in one breath. When she became a little more coherent, Julie gathered that all was not well in the Amiens house. . . ."

Weather conditions never deterred Mère Julie from taking her journeys. At times hail cut her face with the viciousness of steel; at other times snow drifted on her in cold, sponge-like flakes as she trudged up the hill beside the carriage, waiting till she got to the summit before enjoying the little comfort its cheerless interior could give; now the roads are flooded, and the horses are wading flank deep through the mire; all the time she has to endure, as Mère Blin notes, "oaths, impieties, blasphemies, ribald jokes, and sometimes the ribaldry itself. . . ."

We get the speed of decision and the spirit of these journeys in a phrase of Mère Blin's Chronicle:

" Mère Julie received a letter at eleven o'clock one morning. She read it and immediately put on her cloak, hired a cab, sent word to one of the Sisters, who was in class, to prepare herself for a journey which she began to do without any questioning."

We are not concerned to trace the growth of the Institute of Notre Dame, for, in writing the Life of a Foundress, it is only too easy to miss the person of the saintly exemplar in the heaped up chronicle of new and ever increasing foundations. Yet it is here that we can find the clue to the vitality, the undaunted courage, the splendid charity of Julie Billiart. For they are the symbol of what she paid in suffering, in anxiety, "in journeyings often," as the price of these foundations. And, in the midst of all this prayer-filled activity, the shadow of her last great cross came upon her.

She knew that shadow before it came. When all was in sunshine, she said to Mère Blin:

"My daughter, I have still another persecution to go through. It was foretold to me that I should be persecuted by bishops, by priests and *by the Sisters*; all is not over."

Napoleon had usurped teaching authority, and had published *The Universal Catechism of the Empire*, in which occurred the Four Propositions of 1682 and other Gallican errors. The Bishops resisted, and those of Ghent and Tournai were condemned to exile and imprisonment. The Bishop of Namur, however, remained undisturbed, and the rumour went out that he had bowed the knee. This was not the case, for he owed his safety to a certain influence he was able to exercise over the Emperor. Nevertheless a great shadow of suspicion lay on him and, because she was his friend, it claimed Mère Julie also, for she warmly defended him.

"You are not unaware," she writes to the Vicar General of Ghent, "of the troubles which have arisen concerning certain religious opinions and the Universal Catechism. M—— has put into the heads of the young Sisters at G—— some fears that I should adopt the views of my Bishop, whom they accuse of leaning towards the suspected opinions. . . . In Flanders, certain persons have turned against me on account of this; my religious Sisters have been warned about me as if I were likely to lead them into error; in fact, I have borne the most violent attacks without having given any cause for them."

What these "most violent attacks" meant to Mère Julie, we learn from a pathetic sentence in Mère Blin's Chronicle: "Our Mother loved nothing more than peace, but for the purity of the Faith, she would have

sacrificed a thousand lives. I have seen her tears flow
on these occasions." The shadow of this suspicion was
with her to the end.

But a deeper domestic shadow came about her, and
she knew the awful sorrow of a mother who sees her
dearest daughters turning in anger from her. It seems
inevitable in the beginnings of every religious movement that the blight of rigorist views should come temporarily upon it. Notre Dame was not an exception.
Sœur Catherine Daulée, Superior of the Ghent house,
was very wedded to a certain manuscript *Coutumier*,
for the order of the day, arranged by Julie herself, and
she had also some confused ideas about a so-called
"Rule" of the Institute of Mary, which was read to the
Sisters merely as spiritual reading and not as their Rule.
When Mère Julie, then, made some changes in this provisional *Coutumier*, the cry of laxist views was raised
by Sœur Catherine, the intrepid leader who had kept
Montdidier to its allegiance. Then came the unkindest
cut of all when the voice of Sœur Marie Steenhaut, her
first Belgian daughter, and the voice of the well-loved
"Ciska" were heard above the others in the opposition
suddenly loosed against her. From blaming the conduct of their Mother in secret, the Sisters passed to
open discontent. Mère Blin has let us know what the
supposed infractions of religious observance were:
"Mère Julie did not insist that the same thing should
always be done at the same hour if another useful thing
presented itself. The chief end of the Institute being
the teaching of Christian Doctrine, Mère Julie made
no difficulty about entrenching upon what was less important in order to prolong the religious instruction.
In fact she often did so."

At Ghent the daily exercises followed each other in
unchanging order, and this mathematical regularity was
looked upon as essential. It was a clear instance of the
letter of the law taking precedence of its spirit, of

rigidity over-ruling the liberty of the children of God. The prejudices which had arisen in the diocese of Ghent were echoed in that of Tournai and even to some extent in Namur itself; some of the clergy went so far as to suggest dividing the Institute according to the dioceses, in order to separate the Mother-house from Flanders and Hainault. It was then that the Bishop of Namur, at Julie's own request, gave to the Congregation a special ecclesiastical Superior in the person of his Vicar General, the Abbé Médard.

A confidential letter from Mère Blin to Sr. Anastasie Leleu, Superior of Jumet, throws light on this critical period:

"Our Mother is sincerely delighted that all this has been the means of procuring us an ecclesiastical superior. I believe we may congratulate ourselves on the appointment; but whatever is settled between Mère Julie and himself must be accepted by the other dioceses, or things will go on badly. I only wish all had Mère Julie's energy, zeal and forgetfulness of self; there would not be so much fuss about the trifles she is reproached with, if people could understand the excellence of the qualities with which God has endowed her. Our Mother is not troubled on her own account, only so far as the interests of God are concerned; she has no more resentment than an infant."

Julie kept her soul in peace and charity and lifted up with both hands her deep human sorrow to her Master. And with both hands, too, she burned all the bitter accusations and soured affection expressed in many letters that came to her from those she loved best, and in whom she had formed Christ. The pain did its work in her saintly soul and in the souls of her daughters, and all served to throw into stronger light after her death the wisdom of her government and the heroism of her virtue. To quote Mère Blin's words: "This trial was specially permitted by God before He took her to Himself, in order to purify her by so keen a suffering and to bring out her meekness of heart in all its beauty."

Another shadow soon added itself to these, but for her a shadow of joy, a shadow woven of silver and filled with the voices of morning—the shadow of death. In that shadow, she began to speak : grave words that had the wisdom of her years in them. She, about whom the air was clammy once again with misrepresentation and bitterness, spoke of charity. As the Beloved Disciple had done, she went among her Sisters speaking constantly of charity, with the insistence of one who knows her time is short and who would fain have every moment ring with the call that gathered up all the commandments in a command that was like unto the first : " Love ye one another."

In the midst of her labour, the shadows began to lengthen about her. She knew her end was near, and there were a thousand projects in hand. She knew the Hand was raised above her, and lovingly she awaited its stroke of love.

December 7th, 1815, was just a day as any other day, and the Community of Namur went about its duties with that unsung heroism which makes lovely the monotony of convent life. Suddenly there was the noise of a fall on the staircase leading to the chapel. The Sisters rushed to the place and found their Mother lying in a faint at the bottom of the stairs. They were very solicitous for her, but she was quietly insistent, and an hour later she was about her business again. Stabs of headache, pain running like a river through every nerve, could not be ignored, and so Mère Julie was forced to take to her bed. Her pain increased, and the storm of opposition grew in violence. " So people have judged me unfavourably," she writes from her bed of death. " Oh, how good that is to help me to die to my wretched self-love and to the esteem of creatures which I must trample under foot."

Mère Blin was acutely sensitive to the racked soul

of her dearest friend, and there is a sense of pain intimately shared in those words of her Chronicle: "I used often to notice on her countenance an expression of mingled joy and pain. At other times it was all pain, and her glistening eyes told me without words that her soul, too, was suffering."

The shadow of what was perhaps her greatest cross was upon her, and Mère Blin saw its pain in her eyes. For it pleased Christ to give His spouse a share in the soul-searing sorrow in the words: "And they all leaving Him, fled." Not until after her death would those faces of her loved ones be turned again towards her in repentance and love: like her Master, she would die amid the faithlessness of those who had been most faithful, and her resignation and simple trust would be her final offering to her good God.

She had asked for the Last Sacraments at a time when, to all appearances, she seemed quite well. They brought her Lord to her in the Holy Eucharist, and in the fervour with which she received Him, all the prayer and pain, all the struggle and darkness of her life, were lifted up as in a point of splendid love and light. Around her bed knelt her daughters, a sense of loneliness and impending loss upon them, tears streaming down their cheeks. She would live for some time yet, and they would come and go, sorrowful figures moving silently, daughters dreading the loss of a Mother. She was dying in deep peace. The Institute, she said, was God's work and it would live. Of what use was a poor, ignorant peasant woman to it? Others would conserve it, others more worthy would lift it to great heights. There was now but one thing she could do, one thing she could offer in joy. "My dear child," she said to Sister Eulalie, "I am so glad to see the destruction of my nature in homage to its Creator." The soul's thanksgiving, on the threshold of life, for its vesture of clay.

"One day," writes Mère Blin, "as I was preparing to read, as usual, the Imitation of Christ to her, she stretched out her hand and without looking at the book, laid her finger on a verse which she could not possibly see, and said: 'That is the part you must read.' It was the passage: 'If thou carry the cross willingly, it will carry thee, and bring thee to thy desired end, to that place where there will be no end.'"

Had it been the finger of an angel pointing to a text that was to give the shape and meaning of Julie Billiart's life, and the key to its splendour, it could not have chosen a better text. For the Cross lay in great lines of pain on the years of Julie Billiart, and it was fitting that it should shadow her death-bed, that she might clasp it and go with it resplendent before the face of God.

In the midst of their sorrow, a new grief came when, worn out with fatigue, Mère Blin took to her bed, seriously ill. She was anointed and, for a time it seemed that both props were to be taken from Notre Dame. Mère Blin was to be spared, but her recovery was so slow that at Julie's death she was still in a critical condition. She would have herself carried in an arm-chair to Julie's room and they would sit together for the most part in silence.

It was typical of the whole pattern of Julie Billiart's life that there should have been no preparing of the stage for her death, no lowering of the lights, no softening of the music. She died amid the strife and pain in which her life had been led, for an epidemic of fever had broken out in the Convent of Namur; all was bustle and every Sister had an absorbing task to do. Julie had made no fuss, and had asked but one favour—that she might have the burial of the poor and be counted as the least among the Sisters. A great silence had descended on her, and now she rarely spoke. They felt the rhythm of her tremendous prayer in that silence, and they respected it. She had blessed them all and

A KNIGHT OF MALTA GAVE HER AN AUTHENTIC RELIC OF
THE TRUE CROSS

had sent specially, with lovely concern, for a little errand girl in the house who was weeping for her, that she might give her a blessing.

In the increased bustle of sickness in the Convent, she was obtaining what must have been her dearest wish now, that she might turn her face quietly to her God and pass to Him simply and unnoticed.

On Palm Sunday evening, in the quiet of her room, they heard her singing softly and gently to herself, and they knew the wonder of dying lips chanting the Magnificat. As she finished this song of praise that had been so often her inspiration, a profound silence settled on her, and in that silence she went so peacefully to God that the few Sisters present could not tell the exact moment of her death. . . . It was Monday in Holy Week, April 8th, 1816; the shadow of the crucifix rested upon her death even as it had lain upon her life.

Sister Eulalie knelt by the bedside, with a little cruciform reliquary in her hand. Julie had given it to her, that she might die possessed of nothing. The morning sun glistened on it, in a tiny ray piercing the drawn curtains. The morning sun shone on Cuvilly, a little village in Picardy, with the face of an old man: it seeped through the window of the village church and glistened on another reliquary, a more beautiful one, that had once been given to a little child as an unconscious symbol of her years. . . .

They brought Mère Blin to her room, that she might look again on the face of her friend. They left her alone with her great human sorrow. She lifted the cold hand to her lips, and for a long time she remained thus in grief and prayer. Then, raising her head, she looked lovingly in the face of her friend. What she saw caused a great flood of consolation. All pain was gone, Julie's face had the softness of charity in its lines, lips that seemed to smile. Beside that body the tears she shed had nothing of bitterness or discouragement, for through them she looked to the Heaven where she could not but feel that her beloved Mother had become her powerful protectress. Softly in the silence of that room she, too, said the Magnificat.

Mère Julie, clothed in her religious habit, was laid out in the room where she had died on a poor bed, beside which on a little table stood a crucifix between two lighted candles. Around the body knelt the Sisters, at once invoking with the utmost confidence the intercession of her who had so often strengthened them in weakness and consoled them in sorrow. Her limbs remained flexible, the tints of health returned to her cheek, and her lips were parted with a smile, the beauty of which struck all beholders—the smile of a child who dies with eyes fixed upon its Father's face.

As soon as Mère Julie's death became known in the town, many pious persons sent rosaries and medals to touch the body, and begged for pieces of her clothing or of anything which the Servant of God had used. It had been decided that the townsfolk should not be admitted to venerate the mortal remains, but this regulation was impossible to keep; the crowd was so numerous that the great gate of the Convent had to be thrown open in order to satisfy their devotion. "She is a saint," they exclaimed, and the exclamation found its fulfilment when on the feast of St. Joseph, 1906, appeared the Decree of Beatification.

Child of God, Lover of the Cross! So we think of Julie Billiart. And, Holy Church, gathering into her Collects, the substance of her holiness, prays that "through the intercession of Blessed Julie we may ever firmly trust in God in the midst of our earthly trials and by courageous endurance of sufferings attain to the joys of eternity."

THE END